RHINE-GUIDE
from Mainz to Cologne

The Loreley

D1041257

Edm. von König-Verlag, Heidelberg

Contents

The Rhine from Mainz to Cologne

When it gets to Mainz, the Rhine changes direction from north to west, flowing on to Bingen where it is forced through a narrow valley cutting into the slate hills. It took the river millions of years to wear away the 200 - 300 m deep valley. The plateau-like hills are divided into four parts as a result of the deep cuts made by the rivers Rhine, Moselle and Lahn. The rocky Rhine valley was already an important traffic route – on the river and on land – in Roman times. It was from the Romans that the inhabitants learnt how to fortify their towns and, especially important, to cultivate vines on the sunny slopes. After having been elected in Frankfurt, 32 German Emperors and Kings passed through the Middle Rhine area on their way to the coronation in Aachen and showed themselves to the inhabitants there. Ships and rafts were navigated downstream with great difficulty and danger due to the many rapids and reefs, while on shore the travelling merchants were constantly in danger of being attacked by gangs of robbers. When the many castles were built, it became safer to travel by road, but not necessarily cheaper, as the castle owners expected payment in return for protection. Some levied tolls on their own authority, others had the right to charge customs duties as an Imperial fief, so there were ten customs places the merchant had to pay at between Bingen and Koblenz alone. No wonder there was conflict, no wonder many a castle owner was called a robber-baron. Such mischief flourished particularly in the 13th century when the Emperors had very little power, but after 1273 Kaiser Rudolf von Habsburg had the robbers' dens crushed and law and order restored.

Although the castles were originally built to control the owners' property, they also served to protect adjacent settlements. Some castles were also sovereign's residences, thus providing craftsmen, fishermen, farmers and winegrowers with a modest income. With the improvement of firearms in the 16th century, the castles became less significant. Only a few of them, such as Rheinstein and Ehrenbreitstein, were made into fortresses. Many others fell into decay, because the noblemen went to live in more comfortable palaces down in the valley, and were taken over as hiding places by thieves and gangs of robbers. The rest of the castles fell victim to the armies of Ludwig XIV and Napoleon. The only mediaeval castle left standing is the Marksburg.

Goethe's journey down the Rhine in 1774 was the start of the Age of Romanticism. From the beginning of the 19th century onwards, the Rhine valley became a centre of attraction for tourists from many European countries. This sudden interest in the historic ruins meant that attention was paid to preserving the structures and then to the castles being restored from 1825 onwards. Today most of them are open to the public and contain restaurants or museums. What makes this whole area so interesting and attractive for the visitor is not only the large number of castles, but also charming, old-world little towns surrounded by fortified walls, towers and gates, time-honoured churches with artistic burial monuments and neat wine-growing villages framed by sunny vineyards interspersed with steep walls of rock. Year after year millions of visitors are drawn to the romantic Middle Rhine area, which boasts more castles between Rüdesheim and Koblenz than any other region in the world.

Mainz

Even before Christian times there was an open settlement here alongside a walled legionary fortress. This was the headquarters of the Romans in Upper Germania. The «Roman Stones» in the Zahlbachtal (Zahlbach valley) and remains of pillars from their

Mainz: Modern buildings beside the Rhine with the two main spires of the thousand years old Cathedral towering above.

water system are reminders of that period, as are also those parts of the Roman city wall still standing. Boniface, Bishop of Mainz in the 8th century, bestowed on Mainz its important position with regard to this area's conversion to Christianity. Under his successor, Mainz advanced to becoming an archbishopric and was the only town apart from Rome to be granted the name «Holy See». Following this, the archbishops of Mainz were first given the title «Archchancellor of the Empire» (965) and then the chairmanship of the Electoral College (1257). In the 11th and 12th centuries, seven kings were crowned in the Cathedral, the church of the archbishops. For many decades, the citizens of the town put up great resistance to being ruled over by the archbishops, but in 1462 they were defeated by the Elector and Archbishop Adolf von Nassau. From then on Mainz remained the undisputed residence of Electoral Mainz with no self-government by the people. When the Elector fled to escape the French revolutionary troops in 1792, Electoral Mainz became a republic and in 1802 it was deprived of its archbishop's seat. In 1814 Mainz became part

Mainz Cathedral from the north-west. This church combines Romanesque, Gothic and Baroque architecture.

5

Mainz, Cathedral: Archbishops' epitaphs (16th cent.)

of Hessen and in 1950 it was chosen as the capital of the State of Rheinland-Pfalz (Rhineland-Palatinate). The Cathedral **(Dom)**, started under Archbishop Williges (975-1011), is the central point of the Old City. Its monumental size and importance is accentuated by the large squares in the surrounding area and the residences of the wealthy citizens around it. Like the old St. Peter's Cathedral in Rome, it has two transepts. In the fairly small chancel the lower storeys of the slim steeples with their spiral staircases date back to the original church. The Romanesque nave (12th century) connects the transepts, the higher western transept being of great artistic value. The lower floors of the 82.5 m high central tower were completed in 1239, the upper floor as far as the clock added in 1490 and the Baroque top in 1769-74. The architect of the final part was Michael Neumann, son of the famous Balthasar Neumann. The market portal (around 1200), today the entrance to the cathedral, has a two-sided bronze door (around 1000) with an inscription. Thick pillars of mighty blocks of limestone divide the 109 m long church into three aisles. The plain groined vaulting of the nave (29 m high) rises up to the domes of the central towers at a height of 38 and 44 metres.

The cathedral probably contains the best collection of 11th to 20th century epitaphs and statues. The most valuable in artistic terms are the memorial to Archbishop Johann II von Nassau (*1419), with which the so-called «Adalbertmeister» created the typical Gothic Mainz epitaph, as well as the works of the Mainz artist Hans Backoffen from the beginning of the 16th century. The imposing baptismal font of 1328 shows the 12 apostles, the Virgin Mary and St. Martin in relief pewter.
On the market square in front of the cathedral

Renaissance fountain (1526) on the Cathedral Square

the **Renaissance fountain** of 1526 stands out with its magnificent variety of design and colouring. To the east of the cathedral we discover the unique printing museum with its exact reproduction of **Gutenberg's workshop**. Attractive Old City streets full of picturesque half-timbered houses and Baroque aristocratic mansions take us on to the defiant wooden-tower (14th century) to the east and then on to St. Stephan's Church with its impressive cloisters at the southern corner of the Old City. The **Electoral Castle** near the Rhine promenade can be considered one of the finest Renaissance buildings in all of Germany. It is today the home of the Roman-Germanic Central Museum.

The Victor Dativius Arch in the Castle Park provides an attractive view across to the Christuskirche.

Opposite the «Jubilee Fountain» at the south-west corner of the park stands St. Peter's Church. In the centre of the neighbouring «Deutschhausplatz» there is «Jupiter's Column», erected at the time of Roman settlement half way down to their port on the Rhine. The «Deutschhaus» on the northern side of the square is now the home of the state parliament of Rhineland Palatinate. The building standing on the corner where the Deutschhausgasse leads into the square is called the «Sautanz» and is today used by the Südwestfunk broadcasting institution. If we walk along this narrow street, the Deutschhausgasse, we reach the former arsenal, now government offices, with a Stresemann Memorial Hall. Not far away from here is the Natural History Museum.

From among the many events worth mentioning the most outstanding are the Mainz Carnival season with its festive meetings and the traditional Rosenmontagszug (carnival procession on the last Monday before Lent).

The «Wooden Tower» (14th century), one of the gates of the mediaeval town defences.

Wiesbaden

Wiesbaden, the capital of Hessen, owes its name as an international spa and congress centre to its favourable situation as regards transport facilities and to its **hot springs**. The so-called «Kochbrunnen» alone pours out 500,000 litres of warm salt water a day. As early as in the year 50 AD the existence of hot springs was mentioned by a Roman historian. In the following decades Roman baths were built within the settlement, and a wall around them was added about 370. But it was not until towards the end of the 17th century that the town rose to political importance, when the princes of Hessen-Nassau made it their second residence. Then in 1744 when the Nassau sovereign moved his place of residence to the castle of Wiesbaden-Biebrich, he emphasized the importance of his new metropolis.

The spa park borders on the Wilhelmstrasse and the Sonnenbergerstrasse. Near where the two roads meet, the **spa hotel and pump-room,** built in 1907, and the casino used to be the centre of spa activities. The springs and theatre colonnade together with the Hessen State Theatre complete the collection od 19th century Neo-Classical buildings in this area. The modern spa facilities have been moved out to Aukammtal. Opposite the State Theatre, the Burgstrasse leads us into the **Old City**. The slender main tower of the Neo-Gothic market church takes us on to the castle

The spa hotel and pump-room, built in 1907, and the casino used to be the centre of spa activities.

square, dominated by a building which was formerly the Nassau palace and now houses Hessen's State Parliament. The simple façade of the new town hall opposite is livened up by a portico. The old town hall, built in 1609, now serving as the registry office, is the oldest secular building in the town. Sandstone reliefs seem to extend the round-arched windows on the first floor right up to the cornice, thus matching the style of the three entrance doors

Wiesbaden: Market day on Castle Square. To the left of the market church is Hessen's State Parliament, the former Nassau Palace (1840); to the right, behind the lion fountain (1537), stands the new town hall with its portico.

above and beside the outside staircase. The market fountain (1537) in front of the building is decorated with a gold lion bearing his sovereign's coat of arms. Following the Marktstrasse and Langgasse we arrive at the Kranzplatz with the Hochbrunnen, the most famous and most productive of the 27 hot springs in Wiesbaden. The Geisberg on the northern side of the square and the Dambachtal lead us to the **Greek Chapel** – also called Russian Chapel – whose gold domes attract a large number of visitors. It was built on the slopes of the Neroberg between 1848 and 1855 by Herzog Adolph von Nassau as a memorial to his wife Elisabeth Michailowna, who died young. Since 1888, a hydraulic funicular railway has been taking visitors up to the top of Wiesbaden's Hausberg (245 m) with its fine view of the town, as well as to the Opelbad, an open-air swimming pool on the Neroberg.

Hessen's state metropolis offers its visitors the cultured atmosphere of a modern spa town. Apart from the modern spa facilities available, the town naturally also provides its spa guests and other visitors with a wide range of cultural and social events.

Eltville

On the northern bank of the Rhine from Wiesbaden to Rüdesheim we have the delightful Rheingau area, home of the world-famous Rhine wine and one of the most important wine-growing regions in Germany. Passing through the wine-growing village of Walluf we make our way to Eltville, the oldest town in the Rheingau. In the 14th and 15th centuries this was the residence of the archbishops and electors of Mainz. The **castle** was first destroyed in the «tariff war» (1301), was then rebuilt and finally fell a victim to **Swedish** troops in the Thirty Years' War. But the impressive hall-tower, today the home of the Gutenberg Mu-

For many centuries the Electoral Castle in Eltville was the residence of the Archbishops and Electors of Mainz. Its central point is the four-storey Hall Tower (14th century).

seum, with its tower platform and deep dungeon, are still standing. Also worth seeing are the numerous **domains** of court officials.

The Martinstor (St. Martin's Gate) and the Sebastiansturm (Sebastian's Tower) with the remains of the town wall battlements show how well-fortified the town was. The simple **town parish church** is considered to have the most important collection of Late Gothic art treasures in the Middle Rhine area including artistically valuable frescoes, epitaphs, Madonnas and chapels da-

«Burg Crass», a Romanesque nobleman's residence. Behind this the Hall Tower (14th century) of the Archbishops' castle.

ting back to 1400 onwards. The most valuable treasures are the Willigesstein (around 1000), a historical document, as well as the impressive baptismal stone crafted in 1517 in Hans Backoffen's workshop in Mainz. The quaint little streets in the old part of the town around the church are dominated by romantic half-timbered houses and large-scale Baroque buildings.

The towns of **Erbach, Hattenheim, Oestrich** and **Winkel** are lined up on the right bank of the Rhine like pearls on a string. Just before we rech Hattenheim, a road turns off to **Eberbach Monastery** (4 km) founded by Cistercian monks in 1135. With its Romanesque church (12th century) the monastery is considered the most important mediaeval work of art in Hessen.

Hattenheim itself has one of the finest village squares in this part of the country. Besides the old town hall, attractive half-timbered houses and fine domains it also has an imposing ruined tower, the remains of the former castle of 1118.

An old Rhine crane near Oestrich.

Ingelheim: The «Wehrkirche» with the ring-wall was part of the town fortifications in the Middle Ages.

Ingelheim

Halfway between Mainz and Bingen on a site of ancient civilization lies the little town of Ingelheim. Its greatest period in history started with Charlemagne's visit to Nieder-Ingelheim in 774. A Reichsversammlung (Imperial Assembly) was held here in 788, in the course of which Herzog Tassilo of Bavaria was sentenced to death, then pardoned and ordered to spend the rest of his days in a monastery. At about this time, Charlemagne started on the construction of the **Kaiser-Pfalz** (royal residence). The golden age of the Pfalz was under the Saxon kings, who chose it as their residence from 936 to 1043. In 1163 Kaiser Friedrich I «Barbarossa» resided in the Pfalz and had it made into a heavily fortified Reichsburg (Imperial fortress) and a memorial to Charlemagne. It finally lost its importance as a royal residence in 1354 when it became the seat of a collegiate church. A short time later the «Saal» area was made available for settlement. After this the «Reichsburg» had to undergo two stiff tests of its strength, but it both cases – in the sieges by Dieter von Isenburg (1460) and Landgraf Wilhelm II of Hessen (1504) – it proved able to stand up to the test and resist its attackers.

Remains of this probably most important secular building from the early Middle Ages can still be seen today in the evangelical parish church, the **Saalkirche,** first mentioned in 997 as a palace chapel. The figurative and ornamental decoration dates back to the time of the alterations made by Friedrich Barbarossa. The same applies to the unusual chancel. Also still standing are remains of the Carolingian Reichssaal (Imperial Hall) «Aula Regia» and of the outer ring wall with the ruins of the corner tower «Bolander» and a partly walled-up double archway, the Heidesheimer Tor.

The Roman Catholic parish church of **St. Remigius,** built from 1739 onwards in Baroque style, has an impressive Romanesque tower. Whereas the three plain lower storeys were built in the 12th century, the upper storeys and the tympans give evidence of the greater richness in style of the following century.

In the 14th/15th century **Ober-Ingelheim** was the main seat of the Oberhof, the imperial court of appeal. The town's defences with numerous towers and gate-towers are still in good condition, and some parts of the town still give a good impression of what it used to look like, e.g. «An der **Burgkirche**». What really is well worth seeing is the evangelical parish church, which has a ring wall round the fortified churchyard – in places double – and originally formed part of the town's defences, probably also serving as a place of refuge. The guard-house and the battlements of the Staufer church tower (12th century) indicate its significance as part of the town's fortifications. The chancel and the higher extension of the church were added after 1400. In the 15th - 17th centuries, the church was the burial ground of the noble families living in Ober-Ingelheim.

Two of the artistic monuments especially worth mentioning are those of Hans von Ingelheim (*1480) and Wilhelm von Ochenheim (*1465).

Ingelheim: Town wall with a fortified tower near the evangelical parish church (Wehrkirche)

The Niederwald Monument near Rüdesheim

From Rüdesheim and Assmannshausen there is a choice of foot-paths, roads and **cable railways** leading to the top of the Nieder-wald. On the edge of the forest, 225 m above the Rhine, a huge monument designed to symbolize the re-establishment of the German Empire and Germany's unity was erected between 1877

The Niederwald Monument near Rüdesheim: 37.6 m high, erec-ted 1877-83 to commemorate «the re-establishment of the Ger-man Empire».

The Niederwald Monument: bronze relief with the life-size figures of Kaiser Wilhelm I on horseback, Bismarck, the German princes and sovereigns and their commanders-in-chief as well as soldiers from all branches of the armed forces.

and 1883. The main figure on the 37.6 m high monument is the «Germania», 10.5 m tall, bearing the Imperial sword and the German Emperor's crown. 32 tons of bronze were required for casting the weight lady, which greatly accounts for the total cost of 1.2 m gold marks. More than 1 million was donated by the people. The sandstone base has a bronze relief showing nearly 200 life-size figures: Kaiser Wilhelm I on horseback, Bismarck, the German princes and sovereigns and their commanders-in-chief as well as soldiers from all branches of the armed forces. Two angels «War» and «Peace», each 2.8 m high, stand on either side of the statue.

Near the monument there is a breeding and training centre for eagles, which contains a large variety of native birds of prey. From the monument we have a wonderful view across the vineyards right down to Rüdesheim, and across the Rhine to Bingen and Burg Klopp, situated at the mouth of the River Nahe. Looking upstream along the Rhine we see the beautiful Rheingau area; many have sung the praises of this region with its gentle slopes where wine was already being cultivated by Roman veterans 2000 years ago. Looking downstream we see that both the river and the valley become narrower, which marks the beginning of the steep and rugged Middle Rhine section. Well-kept and well-marked footpaths lead into the Niederwald national park, to the hunting lodge or to the St. Hildegard Benedectine Convent (1900-04) with its interesting Beuron-style church and a magnificent view of the Rhine valley from the Convent gardens.

15

Rüdesheim

Just a few kilometres past the town the Rhine abruptly changes direction and becomes narrower. This point, the so-called **Binger Loch,** used to be unnavigable because of its many sandbanks and rapids. So ships going north were unloaded in Rüdesheim, the goods taken to Lorch along the old Celtic road and then put on board ship again there. These re-loading activities brought the town trade and thus a welcome source of income. It was not until the 11th century, when the shipping channel was widened for the first time, that

Cable-railway Rüdesheim-Nieder-wald-Monument. On the right the keep of the Brömserburg.

ships were able to navigate past this extremely dangerous point. But even nowadays it still has its hazards and many navigators from other parts prefer to hire a pilot for the stretch between Rüdesheim and St. Goar. Right next to the Rhine and extending into the water we find the **Brömserburg,** the oldest and best preserved of Rüdesheim's three castles. From the 10th to the 13th century it served the archbishops of Mainz at times as living quarters and as a refuge.

After the archbishops gave it as a fief to the knights «von Rüdesheim» in the 13th century, for a short time it developed into a fearful robber's den. In the Sponheim feud (1281) Archbishop Wernherr von Mainz totally defeated the knights of Rüdesheim and their Sponheim allies. The castle's present name came from the collateral line «Brömser von Rüdesheim», who lived in the castle from 1548 until the line died out in 1668. After 1810 the aristocratic family «von Ingelheim» had it renovated and since then visitors' books have been kept. The oldest such book shows that Goethe stayed there in 1814. Today the castle belongs to the town and houses the Rheingau folk and wine museum with a large collection of drinking vessels.

The **Boosenburg,** formerly called Oberburg, belonged to the Rüdesheim «Füchse» family. The only part still preserved is the defiant castle tower. The market square tower was once part of the Vorderburg, the centrepoint of the inner town defences. In the Oberstrasse we can still see some of the old **aristocratic residences** such as the Ritter'schen Hof (No. 4), the Bassenheimer Hof (No. 5) and the Brömser Hof (No. 27). Heinrich Brömser had the Brömser Hof built in 1542 and decorated with fresco paintings. In the chapel these show a large combined coat-of-arms of the two families Brömser and Greiffenclau, in the ancestral hall there is the «Ahnenprobe» giving evidence of the family's knightly extraction. The coat-of-arms on the courtyard gate was put up around 1650 by Heinrich Brömser, the last male descendant of this aristocratic Rüdesheim family (*1668), court judge and Privy Councillor of Electoral Mainz. Today the Brömser Hof houses «Siegfried's mechanical musical cabinet», a collection of self-playing musical instruments covering three centuries. The Roman Catholic parish church (14th century) on the market square strangely flies a weather-vane with a half-moon and a star. This is said to have been installed by a Ritter (knight) von Brömser, who took part in one of the crusades. In many of Rüdesheim's romantic narrow streets with their cosy wine taverns, many of which sell their own wines, the many visitors can be seen strolling around and stopping to drink a glass of wine or more. One of the most famous streets is the **Drosselgasse.** With

Rüdesheim: Rheinstrasse and Niederwald-Monument.

a population of only 8000, Rüdesheim can accommodate more than 5000 tourists. The town's second most important source of income is wine-growing, in particular the famous Riesling-grape wine, sparkling wines and brandy. The **Adlerturm** (Eagle's Tower) (15th century) at the western end of the Rheinstrasse was once part of the towns' mediaeval defences. The 20.4 m high tower used to be situated right beside the Rhine. It was from here

Rüdesheim: The Brömserburg (around 1000), used in the 13th century by robber-barons as a hiding-place after highway robbery and plundering.

that notice of the first drifting ice was passed on downstream by means of semaphore and fire signals. The ground floor, which has walls one meter thick, used to be a dungeon, only accessible through a first-floor trap-door. A bronze plaque on one of the outer walls commemorates Goethe's visit to Rüdesheim in 1814. The peak season for international tourism in Rüdesheim is from the end of May to the end of October. The highlights of this are the magnificent firework display «The Magic of the Rhine on Fire round the Binger Loch» and the traditional Rüdesheim Wine Festival (mid-August). Wine and Sekt cellars as well as a famous brandy distillery are open to the public on weekdays at any time.

Rüdesheim: The most famous street in the Middle Rhine area, the Drosselgasse. Cosy wine taverns, with and without music, give the visitor a lasting impression of Rhenish hospitality and gaiety. The Drosselgasse is so narrow that, after one glass of wine too many, visitors may find that the walls on the right and left come in handy on their way home.

▲ Mäuseturm and ruins of Ehrenfels   ▼ Drosselgasse

▲ Niederwald Monument   ▼ Rüdesheimer Winzerexpress

▲ *Drosselhof*   ▼ *Mittelalterliches Foltermuseum*

Bingen and Burg Klopp

South of the Nahe mouth on the outer bend of the Rhine lies the ancient city of Bingen. Here, 2000 years ago, the Romans built a citadel they called «Bingium» at an intersection of two trade routes, and the first settlement probably grew up here for reasons of protection. A Christian community is mentioned as early as in the 5th century. In 983, the Emperor Otto II made over this area by the mouth of the Nahe to his Chancellor, Archbishop Williges of Mainz. In the tariff war of 1301, King Albrecht I's troops besieged and conquered Bingen and destroyed its castle. With this war the King broke the power of the Rheinish electors for a few years and forced them to remove the lucrative customs duties levied along the Rhine. But when Albrecht was assassinated in 1308 the levying of duties started up again immediately.

The town's landmark is **Burg Klopp,** situated on a hill in the middle of the town. Probably built in Roman times, it was the seat of noblemen during the period when the archbishops were in power. In the tariff war (1301) the castle troops only surrendered when fire made further defence seem pointless. This gave the castle its title of honour «Burg Klopp the Invincible». After destruction by the French soldiers of Louis XIV in 1689 the castle

Bingen with Bingerbrück on the other side of the River Nahe. In the background, the «Mäuseturm» at «Binger Loch».

Burg Klopp above Bingen. Probably of Roman origin. Today seat of the town council and a folk museum.

had only just been more or less repaired when its owner, the Cathedral Chapter of Mainz had the castle blown up «to prevent its being used as a base in later wars». After 1875 it was rebuilt in the style of 15th century Rhine castles. In 1897 the town bought the castle and since this time it has served as the town hall and a folk museum. Above the gatehouse entrance there is a coat-of-arms of the Cathedral Chapter of Mainz. One of the most interesting things worth seeing in the museum is a collection of Roman doctor's instruments (2nd century).

The foundations of the keep and the 52 m deep castle-well probably date back to Roman times.

Open to visitors: 1.4. to 15.10. daily

View across the Nahe to Bingen and Burg Klopp.

The ruins of Burg Ehrenfels, which once stretched right down to a customs house beside the Rhine. At the mouth of the Nahe, Bingen (left) and Bingerbrück.

The Mäuseturm and the ruins of Burg Ehrenfels

On the Rhine island at Binger Loch the pretty little **Mäuseturm** strikes our eye. It was probably built in the 13th century as a lookout tower for Ehrenfels Castle, which in spite of its towers and outworks had no view of the Rhine to the north. This is where the tower's name came from since «mausen» means to be on the lookout, the way a cat is on the lookout for a mouse. Legend, however, has another interpretation: the hardhearted Bishop Hatto is said to have sought refuge in the tower from a horde of mice; in vain, the mice swam after him and devoured him.

The tower and Ehrenfels castle were partly destroyed by Swedish troops in 1636 and then completely ruined by the French in 1689. The «Romanticist on the Throne», King Friedrich Wilhelm of Prussia, had the base of the outwork propped up and re-

The «Mäuseturm» (13th century), once a lookout-tower for Burg Ehrenfels.

paired and then the tower rebuilt in 1855 in Neo-Gothic style. From then on until 1974 the tower served Rhine navigation purposes as a signal station.

The ruin in the midst of the vineyards above the Mäuseturm is what is left of Burg **Ehrenfels**. The castle, along with its subsidiary buildings, used to stretch right down to the Rhine, the final building right next to the river being the customs house. It was built around 1215 as a customs fortress and passed into the possession of the archbishops of Mainz around 1270. Because of its strategic importance, the archbishops hat it reinforced many times and used it as a hiding place for Cathedral treasures in times of war. Ehrenfels has remained a ruin since it was destroyed by the French (1689). With its mighty curtain wall facing the hillside flanked by towers, it is one of the most impressive constructions along the Rhine.

30 min. walk from Rüdesheim, 15 min. from the level crossing. Beautiful view. Inside not open to the public due to danger of collapse.

Assmannshausen

The romantic village of Assmannshausen, famous for its red wines and situated only a few kilometres downstream from Ehrenfels castle, today is part of the town of Rüdesheim. Built as

The view from the lookout-point «Schweizerhaus» down on to Assmannshausen. The fortified tower of the Late Gothic parish church was the corner-stone of the town's defences.

a Franconian settlement, it was first mentioned officially in 1108 as «Hasemannshusen». A partially preserved ring-wall overlooking the Rhine once served to protect the town from hostile invasion and drifting ice. The cornerstone of the town fortifications was the Late Gothic church guard-tower. The church contains an altar-piece and a madonna, both 15th century works of art.

Assmannshausen: romantic half-timbered house in the town centre.

Along the narrow streets of the town centre picturesque half-timber houses are huddled together, not far from the sun-baked slopes of the «Höllenberg». Here, on the bluish-red phyllite slate of the Taunus area, one of the best German «Spätburgunder» wines is cultivated.

A chair-lift to the Niederwald monument, a hunting lodge and numerous footpaths and splendid vantage points also make the tiny wine-growing village an ideal place to visit, either for a holiday or just for a day out.

Assmannshausen: historical restaurant beside the Rhine.

Burg Rheinstein

Across the Rhine from Assmannshausen Burg Rheinstein with its battlements rises up from a rocky, craggy ridge. Built around 900 as a customs house for the Empire, it was given in about 990 by Emperor Otto III to the archbishopric of Mainz, which had it extended into a fortress. The most significent event in its history was when Kaiser Rudolf von Habsburg sat in judgement upon the «insubordinate» knights of Reichenstein, Sooneck and Ehrenfels. By the 17th century,

Burg Rheinstein: former Imperial custom fortress. First castle to be rebuilt in the 19th century.

the castle had fallen into disrepair and was described as a ruin. Prince Friedrich Wilhelm of Prussia bought it in 1825 and it was one of the first castles he had rebuilt in the following years.
Open (guided tours) daily. Footpath from carpark below the castle 5 minutes, from Trechtingshausen 2 km.

Burg Reichenstein

About 2 km past Burg Rheinstein at the entrance to the town of Trechtingshausen we discover the Clemens Chapel beside the Rhine. Built in the 13th century, this is one of the oldest churches along the Rhine, and on the other side of the Rhine, perched on a rocky ridge, we see Burg Reichenstein, one of the oldest castles (11th century). In 1253 this robber knight's castle was destroyed by the Rheinischer Städtebund (Rhenish Town Alliance). In 1282 Rudolf von Habsburg had this robber's den destroyed again and the robbers executed near the Clemens Chapel. In 1899 it was bought by Baron von Kirsch-Puricelli and renovated.

Like Ehrenfels Castle, Burg Reichenstein also has a mighty curtain wall flanked by two towers instead of a central keep. This wall is 8 m thick at its base, 5 m thick at the top and 16 m high. Inside there is now a hotel-restaurant. The other rooms contain valuable furniture and a remarkable collection of arms and antlers.

Open to the public (guided tours) January - October. Carpark in castle yard. Footpath from the Rhine 5 min.

Castles Sooneck, Heimburg and Fürstenberg

The village of Trechtingshausen, which is well worth seeing, still possesses remains of a medieval sentry wall on the Rhine, a romantic gate in Neuweg and a crenelated round tower. Just as Reichenstein, situated above the village, so the neighbouring castle of Sooneck also belonged to robber bands and which were destroyed on two occasions during

Burg Reichenstein (11th century) above Trechtingshausen.

Castle Sooneck near Trechtingshausen. Built in the early 11th century. Twice destroyed as a nest of robber barons in 1253 and 1282.

the 13th century. The emperor lifted a temporary ban on building in the year 1349 and the new owner Kurmainz, had the castle re-erected. In 1689, it fell vic tim to storming French troops and in the 19th century, Crown Prince Friedrich Wilhelm of Prussia commissioned it to be rebuilt in the romantic style. The sleepy village of Niederheimbach lies sprawled out on its narrow stretch of bank on the Rhine, and just a little above its roofs one perceives Kurmainz Heimburg in all its splendour, built in or about 1300 as a northern bastion against the territories of the dukes of the Palatine. Later, the castle fell into decay, but was rebuilt in the 19th century. One notices with interest the strong, ivy-bedecked curtain walling and the 25 metre high keep. Castle Fürstenberg above Rheindiebach was erected by the Archbishop of Cologne both to protect his property and also his right to exact duties and taxes in the year 1200. It has remained in ruins since its destruction in 1689. The tapered keep, crowned by crenelated battlements is still in good condition.

Conducted tours of Burg Sooneck only from March to September. The way there on foot is about one kilometre.

Lorch

On the opposite side, where the River Wisper joins the Rhine, we find the wine-growing town of Lorch below the Nollich ruins (pre-1100). The Gothic parish church (started in the 13th century) contains ancient epitaphs and an artistically styled high altar.

Bacharach

Together with Burg Stahleck, Bacharach became part of Count
Palatinate property in the 11th century. Its important wood and
wine trade as well as its customs duties made Bacharach alongside Kaub one of the wealthiest towns in the whole of the Palatinate. The **town fortifications** (14th century) are the best preser-

*Bacharach: The well-preserved towers of the town's mediaeval
fortifications, St. Peter's parish church (from 1100 onwards), the
ruins of the Werner Chapel (1294) and Burg Stahleck are the
sights most worth seeing.*

ved in the Middle Rhine area together with those of Oberwesel.
It is possible to walk along the whole length of the sentry walk on
the Rhine front, seven of the towers are still fully preserved, even
the connenting wall to the castle as a kind of corner-stone is still
standing. The former customs bastion jutting out into the Rhine
at the southern end of the town was converted into a Capuchin
monastery around 1700, and the church of this monastery is still
standing. The main St. Peter's Church was built in around 1100
and contains valuable mediaeval frescoes.
There are many **half-timbered façades** to be admired, of which
perhaps the old Post Office, with its splendid courtyard, and the
«Old House» (1568) on the market square are most worthy of

mention. Halfway up to the castle we find the striking ruins of the Gothic **Werner Chapel,** which was built from 1294 onwards over a period of 140 years. The district of **Steeg,** 1 km away from the Rhine, has not only a large number of picturesque half-timbered houses but also an interesting 14th century church with mediaeval frescoes. In former times Burg Stahlberg (13th century), watched over Steeg and the valley; today the castle is in ruins.

Burg Stahleck

There has been documentary evidence of Lords of Stahleck Castle since the beginning of the 12th century. In 1142 Hermann von Stahleck became Count Palatinate. In the following decades he and his successors completed the «Palatinate Barrier», consisting of the castles of Gutenfels, Pfalzgrafenstein, Stahleck, Stahlberg and Fürstenberg.

Bacharach: the «Old House» (1568), one of the many picturesque half-timbered houses in the old part of the town.

Burg Stahleck above Bacharach, seat of the Count Palatine in the 12th century and important corner bastion against the other Rhenish Electors.

This meant that this strategically important area where four territories of the Rhenish Electors met was more or less secure. Burg Stahleck was rebuilt after the Thirty Year's War, only to be wrecked again by French troops in 1689. The «Rheinischer Verein» (Rhineland Association) had it restored on its old foundations in 1925-27 as a youth hostel. The basic construction of the round keep in the middle of the castle yard dates back to the 12th century. The 14th century ring-wall becomes stronger on the side of attack to form a curtain wall flanked by corner towers. The entrance to the castle yard leads across a bridge – formerly a drawbridge – through the outer castle gate, the outer bailey and the inner gate. The keep (Palas) on the eastern side with its mighty hip-roof was reconstructed in 1931. The half-timbered buildings are still used as a youth hostel.

Car park. Footpath from Bacharach 25 min. Open by arrangement.

Bacharach: the ruins of the Gothic Werner Chapel (from 1294 onwards). On the right St. Peter's parish church (from 1100).

Kaub with the «Pfalz» and Burg Gutenfels

The town was first mentioned in 983 when it fell to the Arch-bishopric of Mainz. At the beginning of the 13th century the town, the right to collect customs duties on the Rhine and the castle – then mentioned for the first time – were in the hands of the Herren (Lords) von Falkenstein, who, however, sold their property to the Palatinate in 1277, which Kaub remained part of until 1802. In 1326 King Ludwig der Bayer («the Bavarian») resided in the castle. Around this time the island fortress **«Pfalzgrafenstein»** – in short «Pfalz» – must already have been under construction, as a year later Pope John XXII called on the archbishops of Mainz, Cologne and Trier to destroy the tower erected on an island on the Rhine near Kaub. A stone memorial tablet on the former Palatinate town hall commemorates the successful defence of Kaub in 1504, when the castle and town were besieged for 6½ weeks by the Landgrave Wilhelm von Hessen. The valiant way the castle was defended gave it the name **«Gutenfels»**. It also gave rise to the legend and the historical play about «Elslein von Kaub». Kaub's fateful hour came on New Year's Eve 1813/14 when the Prussian Field Marshal **Blücher** crossed the Rhine here in pursuit of Napoleon.

Burg Gutenfels above Kaub. On the Rhine island «Falkenaue», the former customs bastion Pfalzgrafenstein, called «Pfalz».

The «Pfalz» near Kaub, with Burg Gutenfels in the background.

*Kaub: The Blücher Memorial on the Rhine Promenade symboli-
zes Napoleon's being «thrown out» of Germany 1813/14. Above
the legendary «marshal Onwards» stands Burg Gutenfels
(around 1200).*

The Blücher Museum in his former quarters at 6, Metzgergasse
is open to the public every day except Monday and contains a
collection of arms and uniforms from that period. The Blücher
memorial owes its location on the Rhine promenade to a natural
disaster: a landslide in 1876 cost 26 lives and wrecked 10 houses

but it left behind a wider bank along the Rhine. Beside the memorial stands the Kaub water-level registration tower. Part of the mediaeval fortifications are still standing, e.g. the «Round Tower» in the east of the Old Town. At the western boundary of Old Kaub we find the Romanesque Wesel gate-tower. In the town itself the romantic streets «Auf der Mauer» and «Metzgergasse» as well as the Palatinate town hall with its coat-of-arms of the Electoral family are worthy of mention. The evangelical and Roman Catholic church under one roof grew up out of a late Romanesque church building. Until 1770 the Catholics celebrated their Mass in the chancel but then this was replaced by a new building in Late Rococo style. On a rocky crag behind the church is perched the bell-tower.

Customs duties being levied in Kaub were first mentioned in 1257. At that time there was a customs house on the flat Rhine island «Falkenaue». The five-sided, six-storey tower of the **«Pfalzgrafenstein»,** a castle built as a customs house in the middle of the Rhine, was started in about 1325; from 1340 onwards a 12 m high ring-wall in the shape of a ship's hull was put up around it. The outer wall shows a stone lion bearing the coat-of-arms of the Palatinate. Behind this there are gun bastions and several-storeyed wooden arcades with a sentry-walk. A portcullis in the ring-wall additionally fortified the entrance. Even today the entrance to the tower is on the third floor. What is especially interesting is the old castle dungeon, the floor of which could be raised and lowered depending on the water level.

Open to the public March - October, except Monday.

Above the «Pfalz» rises up the older of the two castles, **Burg Gutenfels,** built around 1200 by the Falkenstein family. It was in the King's Hall in 1287 that Burgrave Adolf von Nassau received news of the fact that he had been chosen to succeed Rudolf von Habsburg as king. A mural painting in this room depicts the announcement of this by heralds. The main construction with a 35 m high keep, the Palas (living quarters), the armoury and the inner castle yard is well preserved. The ring-wall dates back to the 14th century. In 1806 Napoleon had the castle defences removed and the castle put up for auction to be demolished. An archivist prevented its complete demolition by buying the ruins. After 1888 the architect Walter had it rebuilt. Today it is considered one of the most attractive and spacious castles along the Rhine and is the home of a hotel.

3 km footpath and road from Kaub. Not open to the general public.

Schönburg Castle and Oberwesel

Within view of Kaub the little town of Oberwesel snuggles into a little opening of the Rhine Valley. Surrounded by gently sloping vineyards, the town and its tower defences is proud of its appropriate nickname «town of many towers and wine». High above its silhouette, the majestic, thousand year old **Schönburg** keeps watch over the town. At one time the possession of the Grafen (Counts) von Stahleck, it was given in 1166 by Friedrich I «Barbarossa» to one of his officials as an imperial fief. He and his descendants then called themselves «von Schönburg» after the name of their residence. The customs duties on the Rhine in Oberwesel made them one of the richest and most powerful families in this region. 100 years after the granting of the fief, five families with the name «von Schönburg» already lived in the fortress, and in the 14th century it was extended into a spacious family castle called Ganerbenburg. It remained in this family until it was destroyed by the troops of King Louis XIV «Le Roi Soleil». After 1885 its owners had it partly rebuilt. Since then one part of the spacious castle has been used as and International Youth Hostel, another part as a hotel.

Footpath from Oberwesel 30 minutes. Car park beside the castle. Open to the public daily.

An impressive part of the structure is the mighty curtain wall on the side of the castle looking uphill. Behind this wall the division into three parts, with two keeps and one tower with living quarters, is clearly recognizable.

Schönburg Castle near Oberwesel. Its owners, the Lords of Schönburg, had it extended into a spacious family residence after 1166.

The **town** itself is situated on the site of an old Celtic settlement (400 BC) and a Roman military service point. In 1237 Schönburg Castle became subject to the Emperor alone, and Oberwesel, formerly Wesel, was able to pay 300 marks in silver and thus rid itself of Schönburg rule. In this way it became a free imperial town. In the following years the circumvallation was replaced by a city wall; with its 18 towers it is the most complete city wall still standing in the whole Middle Rhine area. Its massive solid round towers beside the Rhine, the Ochsenturm (Oxen Tower) and the

Oberwesel has the most complete and best-preserved mediae-val town fortifications in the Middle Rhine area. It has 18 fortified towers still standing. Rising up above the roofs of the town the Gothic churches of St. Martin (right) and «Liebfrauen» (Church of Our Lady).

Haagsturm are particularly worth seeing. The dainty little Werner Chapel and the now-ruined Franciscan monastery were also built in the same century. After 1300, with the help of the wealthy **Herren** (Lords) von Schönburg, the two Gothic collegiate churches «Liebfrauen» (Our Lady) and «St. Martin» were built, both of which contain valuable works of art, signs of the wealth of the town. The famous organ in the slender Liebfrauenkirche is especially worth mentioning.

The Loreley

Still today, mention of the Romance of the Rhine conjures up a picture of the mighty slate rock between Kaub and St. Goarshausen called the Loreley. Downstream the river was squeezed into its narrowest and deepest point; even in the 19th century, reefs and rapids made it extremely dangerous for ships and rafts to pass this point, so a «three bells» warning told the crew it was time to pray. Moreover the rock was already famous in the early

View of the narrow valley of the Middle Rhine area. The most striking point is the steep, outjutting «Loreley» rock in the centre of the picture.

Middle Ages for its good echo, thought to be ghostly voices. No wonder a multitude of legends was woven around the rock, the most famous of which is that of siren called «Loreley», who bewitches the hearts of sailors with her unearthly beauty and her enchanting voice. The sailors look up at the rock to catch sight of

The «Loreley»: The legendary slate rock rises up almost verti-cally to 132 m above water-level.

the charming maiden, forgetting for just a moment the danger-ous rapids and reefs. Their boat is dashed to pieces and they sink beneath the waves for ever. This is what happened also to the young Erbgraf (heir to the Count's title) von Rheinpfalz, who is lured to his doom in this way. His father orders that the witch on the rock be caught or killed. When soldiers bar the way back into her cave, she calls on her father, the Rhine, to help her. Huge, foaming waves rise up out of the waters and carry the maiden away. Since then she has never been seen again. But sometimes, when the moon is shining bright, a mysterious singing is to be heard, described by Romanticist poets. Heinrich Heine's Song of Loreley, set to music by Silcher, made the Loreley Rock famous all over the world.

There is a footpath up to the top of the rock from the car park at the foot of the Loreley; alternatively the road can be taken from St. Goarshausen right up to the peak. A magnificent and unfor-gettable view is to be had from here of some of Germany's most famous scenery. The well-kept outdoor theatre from the Third Reich is used for many different events. Near the Berghotel we see the remains of a rampart originally part of a Celtic place of refuge.

Burg «Katz»

The siren «Loreley», who lured sailors to their doom with her unearthly beauty and her bewitching singing.

After the Counts of Katzenelnbogen had built Burg Rheinfels above St. Goar in the middle of the 13th century, they then had «Neukatzenelnbogen» Castle, «Katz» for short, erected on the other side of the Rhine in 1371. It served to reinforce Rheinfels Castle, safeguarded the crossing-point to its training-grounds, defended the little town of Hausen, and made it possible to give early warning of ships coming round the Loreley. With its «sister» it thus provided an effective barrier across the river above all aimed at defending its right to levy customs duties. The steep walls of the rocky ledge the castle stands on provided protection on three sides. On the side towards the hill, the Counts had a deep moat hewn into the rock. The stone bridge, which led into the long bailey, could be blown up in times of war. The side open to attack was also protected by means of a 40 m high keep. Strong fortified walls connected the keep on both sides with the living quarters, the five-sided Palas, across the protective steep hillside. The thick outer walls of the Palas as well as a slightly lower triangular bastion in front of it additionally fortified the castle, which was very likely impregnable before the arrival of firearms. The three-storey Palas contained not only the Burggrafenstufe and a number of lady's rooms and chambers but also two magnificent halls. From the benches within the projecting round towers the inhabitants had to splendid view of the river and the town. In the storage-cellars was the wine that added spice to the banquets. From the halls there were doors to the sentry walks and from there to the keep, which was a final place of refuge in case of emergency. Only the ground floor, the castle dungeon, could be reached from the courtyard. A spiral staircase let into the wall overlooking the courtyard connected the five upper storeys. The octagonal top floor with its look-out bays was the tower guards' abode. The other floors were inhabited and even had a fire-place. The keep and the staircase up the side of the Palas as well as the building for the kitchen and the bakery took up quite a lot of space within the fortified walls, in addition to which there was the well for drinking water in the centre of the courtyard.

The defending troops consisted of the commander (called Burg-graf – burgrave – in the Middle Ages) and 50 to 80 mercenaries. In times of crisis reinforcement was called for and the citizens of the town were required to accommodate and feed the troops free of charge. Napoleon had the castle blown up in 1806, but it was rebuilt at the turn of the century. Later extensions by various owners changed the original mediaeval appearance of the castle. Today it is a convalescent home.

Footpath from St. Goarshausen 20 min. Open on request.

Burg «Katz» above St. Goarshausen, started in 1393 in order to reinforce the main castle «Rheinfels» opposite.

St. Goarshausen

The fishing village of St. Goarshausen became the property of the powerful Grafen von Katzenelnbogen in 1284. Soon after it became a town (1324), the 200 or so inhabitants started to erect a fortified town wall. On the side next to the Rhine they built a 230 m long, 11 m high construction, which also protected them

St. Goarshausen with Burg Katz: the magnificent firework display and Bengal illuminations called «The Rhine on Fire» (Rhein in Flammen).

from flooding and drifting ice. The east tower and the market tower are still standing. They flanked the Rhine promenade and shielded the two town-gates at the same time. From here the walls went uphill and with the «Katz» formed a defence triangle. The town itself consisted of two rows of houses on either side of the only road there was room for between the river and the rocky hillside. Still today there are attractive half-timbered houses in the «Grosse Burggasse». Houses no. 41-43 were originally the town hall (1532), which also housed the school and a teacher's flat. The square in front, called the Plan, was the market place and as such the centre of social life in the town. At no. 44 a slate flight of steps branches off, leading to the old church and the churchyard. On the round market tower there is an unusual weather vane. The tower stands on the alluvial land of the Forstbach (forest brook) and over the years it has developed into the «leaning tower of St. Goarshausen». It is now inclined at an angle of 41 cm to the east and as much as 63 cm to the north. The square east tower was built directly on the rocky banks and was originally 23 m high. When the road was built, however, the surface level was raised, so that now the former ground floor with the dungeon is below ground and the entrance to the first floor is now on ground level. The four inhabitable storeys of the tower were burnt out in 1873.

4 km from St. Goarshausen on the slopes of the Hasenbachtal (Hasenbach Valley) we find the **Reichenberg** ruins (14th century), of great importance in castle history. It is the Katzenelnbogen family's third castle in this area. A wide curtain wall is flanked by two round towers. The remains of the 3-storey Palas (Hall building) have an almost classical appearance due to the fact that the ceilings have collapsed and three times three pillars left standing on top of each other bearing a high ribbed vault.

No viewing inside due to danger of collapse

St. Goarshausen: Walk along the Rhine Promenade, in the background Burg «Neukatzenelnbogen», called «Katz» for short.

View of Burg Katz, with St. Goar and Burg Rheinfels in the background.

St. Goar

The sister towns of St. Goarshausen and St. Goar are connected by a car ferry. Both owe their name to St. Goar, who lived as a hermit in the 6th century where the collegiate church of St. Goar now stands on the site of the chapel he built. By 765 the Saint's hermitage had grown into one of Germany's oldest monasteries. In the 12th century the Katzenelnbogen family acquired control of the monastery and the settlement as well as the right to levy duties on the Rhine in St. Goar. Being a fortified town, it was often involved in military conflicts such as the unsuccessful sieges of 1255/56, 1320, 1322, as well as several times in the Thirty Years' War and particularly in the Seven Years' War when altogether 81 houses, the hospital and the town hall were wrecked as a result of an explosion (1759) and arson by Irish soldiers (1761).

From the battlements of the **Stiftskirche** (Collegiate Church) the militia marksman Kretsch came up with a legendary bull's-eye when he wounded the French General Tallard so badly that his troops stopped the siege.

Beneath the chancel of the Stiftskirche is the Goarskapelle, a popular place for pilgrims until the Reformation. The inside of the church is decorated with Gothic mural paintings and delicate net vaulting, a beautiful pillar pulpit and three magnificent monuments to the Landgraf (landgrave) Philipp II von Hessen-Rheinfels

St. Goar: View of the Stiftskirche (started in 1444). Of the original 8th century church the tomb of St. Goar is still preserved.

and his wife and also to Countess Adelheid von Katzenelnbogen (*1329). The smaller Roman Catholic parish church contains a 14th century Goar epitaph, which once served as a tombstone in the Goarkapelle. A Gothic triptych (around 1470) from the school of the «Hausbuchmeister» forms the centrepiece of the valuable high altar. The bell-tower is the former Koblenzer Tor (Koblenz Gate) containing a second Goar piece. The only parts of the town wall still standing are on the side towards the hill, towered over by the Hexenturm (Witches' Tower) and the Kanzleiturm (Chancellor's Tower).

Once a year on the third Saturday in September the two towns arrange a magnificent firework display called **«Rhein in Flammen»** (The Rhine on Fire). The towns and their castles are illuminated by Bengal lights and fireworks are set off from the castle towers.

Mediaeval depiction of St. Goar

St. Goar with its harbour and the castle ruins of Rheinfels. Opposite the sistertown of St. Goarshausen with Burg Katz.

Burg Rheinfels

Construction of the main structure of the castle was started in 1245 by Graf Dieter V von Katzenelnbogen. Only ten years later it was able to stand its first test when it was attacked by 9000 soldiers of the Rheinischer Städtebund (Rhenish Town Alliance) because of an increase in customs duties on the Rhine. After 40

Model of Rheinfels fortress according to plans of the surveyor Dilich, made in 1607. On the left the basic castle and the residential buildings, on the right towards the hillside the extensive fortifications.

unsuccessful charges and a siege lasting more than a year they were forced to withdraw empty-handed. When the powerful Katzenelnbogen family died out, the landgraves of Hessen acquired Rheinfels Castle in 1479, and from the 15th century onwards they added outworks and underground passages to fortify it as well as new living quarters. In the Palatinate War of Succession, Rheinfels Castle with 4000 men was the only fortress along the Rhine to withstand in 1692/93 the assault of a French army of 28,000 troops with 56 pieces of artillery. In 1758 the meanwhile neglected castle fell into enemy hands for the first time when the soldiers capitulated to French troops without a fight. Again in 1794, despite the fact that he was well equipped and had 3200 men under arms, a weak commander surrendered the fortress without a struggle which then fell into the hands of poorly-armed French revolutionary forces. He was later sentenced to death for this. In 1797/98 the French blew up the fortifications and the castle. The ruins were used as a quarry to provide stones for the rebuilding of Ehrenbreitstein fortress near Koblenz for example, until the Prince of Prussia bought it in 1843 and saved it from falling into complete decay.

A walk around the extensive ruins with their maze of several-storey sentry walks and underground passages gives us an excellent impression of the one time most powerful fortress along the Rhine. The underground passages beneath the outworks were filled with gunpowder in times of war so that they could be blown up along with any enemy troops that managed to penetrate the fortifications. This happened in 1626 to 300 Spanish soldiers from the army of the von Hessen-Darmstadt family. A look around the well-equipped **Burgmuseum** also gives a good idea of the former size of the whole construction. A model of the fortress in the former chapel shows clearly how strong its defensive position was, especially on the north side which was the main side of attack. It was possible to reconstruct the buildings exactly because in around 1607 a land surveyor called Schäfer, known as Dilich, was commissioned by Landgrave Moritz to make detailed drawings in colour along with sectional views and lay-out plans of the whole structure.

Open to the public April - October, with or without guided tours. Tours last 1¼ hours. Car park next to the castle. Climb up from St. Goar 10 min.

Original Tower of Rheinfels ruins and High Battery.

Rheinfels: View of the castle with its high Darmstädter Bau.

Burg Maus above Wellmich

Within view of Burg Katz and situated above St. Goarshausen-Wellmich stands Burg **«Maus»**. It was given this nickname because its neighbour Katz (cat) Castle was owned by the powerful Katzenelnbogen family, who only seemed to be waiting for a favourable opportunity to pounce on the «Maus» (mouse). The castle, which was completed in 1356 under the Archbishop of Trier Kuno von Falkenstein, was considered one of the most advanced and best fortified in its time. The Thurnburg or Theuerburg, to use its proper name, for a time was the residence of the

Burg «Maus» above Wellmich. The Electoral Trier castle «Thurnberg» (1356) was given this name because of its proximity to Burg «Katz».

archbishops of Trier. Napoleon had it blown up in 1806 as part of his campaign to destroy all of the Rhine fortifications. Fortunately the magnificent structure was rebuilt in 1900-1906 in accordance with the original plans.

The almost square outer wall widens on the side towards the hill, where the moat is, into a curtain wall, surpassed by the mighty

round keep near the outer wall. Opposite it is a four-storey tower with living quarters. Here, as well as in the imposing Palas (Hall) next to it, corner-bays emphasize the excellent fortifications of the whole structure. Together with the dainty round-arch frieze, they are at the same time attractive decorative elements within a harmoniously designed construction. The valuable interior with its extensive collections from the time of the reconstruction of the castle make it really worth a visit. The splendid view of the Rhine valley also makes up for the steep climb.
Open on request. Road up from Wellmich. Footpath 25 min.

The small town of **Wellmich** is today part of St. Goarshausen. It already had the statuts of a town when the castle was completed in 1356. At about the same time the Gothic parish church was built, one of the most beautiful in the Middle Rhine area, with a wonderful chancel. One of the most interesting Late Gothic statues in the church is a Pietà (around 1450). A magnificent fresco showing the Day of Judgement also dates back to the 15th century. On the outer wall of the vestry there is a painted sandstone masterpiece of the Crucifixion.

Downstream, opposite Hirzenach, we see the parish of **Kestert**. From here there are footpaths up to the look-out point called Hindenburghöhe. Further down the Rhine we pass through the small town of Bad Salzig, a well-known spa with thermal springs and a modern spa clinic.

View of Bad Salzig, a spa with hor springs.

Kamp-Bornhofen and the «Hostile Brothers»

Passing the castles of Sterrenberg and Liebenstein, known as «the hostile brothers», we arrive at Kamp-Bornhofen. On the way up to the castles, we pass **Kloster Bornhofen** (1679-84). The old 13th century pilgrims' church was given its present appearance at the beginning of the 15th century. A Passion picture shows members of Rhenish aristocratic families as sponsors and donors. At the beginning of the 20th century, when the

Kamp-Bornhofen and the «hostile brothers» Sterrenberg and Liebenstein. Below the Wallfahrtskirche and Kloster Bornhofen.

church was no longer able to accommodate all the pilgrims, the Franciscan monks had a beautiful pilgrims' place laid out on the north side in 1912, and then, in 1932/33 an even larger one with room for 5,000 pilgrims.

The one time rich contents of the monastery were given by the Herzog (Duke) von Nassau in 1813 to the parish of St. Boniface in Wiesbaden. The only thing left was the Miraculous Image. The partly whitewashed Burg **Sterrenberg** came into existence in the

11th century as a Reichsburg. In 1248 the Burggraf von Sterrenberg had the wooden house 30 m above the fortress extended into an outwork which later bacame Burg **Liebenstein**.

At the same time the burgrave had the 2.5 m thick outer curtain wall between the castle and the outwork put up. Although this was originally intended to improve the defences of both castles, at first sight it seems to be directed menacingly against Liebenstein Castle. This gave the wall its nickname «wall of conflict». The second castle also has a moat and fortified walls with embrasures on the side facing Sterrenberg Castle. No wonder people gave the castles the nickname «the hostile brothers». Sterrenberg Castle was protected on three sides by its location on top of a rocky crag; the fourth side was for-

Miraculous Image in the Wallfahrtskirche in Bornhofen, the destination of many pilgrims since the 13th century.

tified with two curtain walls, a moat and gates. Nevertheless the buildings were described as being in decay as early as 1568 and used as a quarry. Recent modifications have made it possible for the two castles to be used as restaurants. The «Sterrenberg» received its original colour a few years ago – white with red brickwork.

Burg Sterrenberg, built as an Imperial Castle in the 11th century. The outer curtain wall looking towards the former outwork Liebenstein has the nickname «wall of conflict».

Kamp-Bornhofen. «Der von der Leyensche Hof», a typical Rhenish Renaissance building.

After the line of the «Schenken von Liebenstein» had died out, the earlier castle went in 1783 as Nassau fief to Baron «von Preuschen» whose successors still own it.

Both castles open to the public daily. Car parks near the castles. Footpath from Bornhofen 30 min.

The district of **Kamp** was first mentioned in 1138, and until about 1315 it was subject to the Emperor alone. Then the town and the castles passed into the possession of Electoral Trier until 1802. The town centre has many historic half-timbered houses, especially in the Rheinuferstrasse and Kreuzstrasse. Of the mediaeval St. Nicholas parish church (1251) only the tower remains standing; the rest had to make way for a new building in Neo-Gothic style in 1902. The pulpit, however, was part of the original church. Opposite the main door of St. Nicholas' Church we see the beautiful portal of the Augustinian convent with a statue of St. Augustine. The date shown (1732) is the year in which the original convent was renovated as it stands today. The convent itself was dissolved in 1802. In the Schmiedgasse we find the «Von der Leyensche Hof», a typical example of Rhenish Renaissance.

Boppard

Diagonally across from Kamp-Bornhofen, just before the narrow horse-shoe bend in the Rhine lies the old Imperial town of Boppard. In the 4th century the Romans replaced their citadel by a stone fortress with 28 towers, which, however, was soon overrun by Germanic tribes. Today no other German town has such well-preserved Roman fortress ruins as Boppard. The former Free Imperial City was subjugated in 1327 by the elector Balduin von Trier, after King Heinrich VII had pawned it away to his brother, the Elector, 15 years earlier. Balduin immediately had the Electoral Trier castle built, thereby forcing the uncooperative inhabitants to accept his rule. A walk around this extremely interesting town could well at the **Carmelite Church** (started in 1319) in the Rheinallee. It contains two 17th century altars, numerous tombstones of local noble families, and a statue of the Virgin Mary (1330) called the «Traubenmadonna». The 5th century tombstone of a child's grave, the so-called «Armeniusstein», is one of the oldest Christian monuments. The Baroque building further up was completed in 1730 as a monastery and is now used by the

Boppard, an old Imperial Town, with well-preserved remains of a Roman city wall (4th century). The chair-lift goes up to the lookout-point «Vierseenblick».

town council. The cloisters surround a spacious courtyard with an attractive Germanic pillar fountain. The Karmeliterstrasse and the Oberstrasse take us on to the Kirchgasse. The Gothic archway to the left once belonged to the «Danzhus» (15th century). At the Angertstrasse junction we discover on the right-hand side parts of the Roman wall with the remains of a tower. We follow the road on the left to the Binger Tor, part of the mediaeval town fortifications. Up on a hill we see the Baroque building of the former Marienburg Convent (1740). The Casinostrasse leads us down the Rheinallee, which takes us back into town. A strong wall, called the «Eisbrech» (Icebreaker) used to con-

Boppard by night. The St. Severus Church (1150-1326). The floor of the church contains the outline of the baptismal font and the pulpit of the original 5th century church.

nect the Sandtor with the river. The Gothic town hall next to it was once inhabited by the Ritter von Schwalbach, whose tombstones we noticed in the Carmelite Church. We walk past the former Franciscan monastery (17th century) and a stately Baroque house with a coat-of-arms on the balcony railing. All that is left of the original Electoral Trier castle is the keep. The tombstones and the statue in the inner courtyard are from St. Severus Church. The castle today houses a folk museum. Behind the castle is the

The «Vierseenblick» (view of four lakes) from the lookout point above Boppard. On the left beside the hill on the bend lies Osterspai.

Burggasse we discover 15 m of the old **Roman wall** by the **Römerburg»** Hotel. Continuing along the Untere Marktstrasse we arrive at **St. Severus Church,** which contains a painted ceiling from around 1200 as well as an artistically valuable triumphal cross above the altar (13th century). The Kronengasse and Kronentor then take us past picturesque half-timbered houses and back to the Rheinallee.

A cable railway goes up to one of the most famous look-out points along the Rhine, the **«Vierseenblick»,** overlooking four lakes at once. On our way up and down we have a wonderful view of the biggest horse-shoe bend along the Rhine.

The big horse-shoe bend near Boppard. The railway and the road follow the river round the hill on the bend.

Braubach and the Marksburg

Leaving Boppard, the river, the roads and the railway wind round a narrow horse-shoe bend. At the end of the steep right-hand bend lies the village of Osterspai with its small, fortified 13th century castle. The tower containing living quarters, which was added in the 14th century, is still standing today. The Ba-

Braubach and Marksburg fortress (12th century). The dark, solid tower in the middle of town was once part of the town's mediae-val fortifications; since the 14th century it has been part of the Early Gothic St. Barbara's Church.

roque castle above the village is called Liebeneck (17th century). At Spay, on the left-hand side, after a left bend, the Rhine regains its northwesterly direction. On a wooded peak on the right-hand side stands the imposing Marksburg above the town of **Braubach.** Burial grounds indicate that this area has been inhabited since about 500 BC. It was first mentioned in the 7th century. The Herren von Eppstein, who had been given a Palatinate fief, built the castle and were the owners of the town in the 12th century. Their successors in 1283 were the powerful Grafen von Katzen-elnbogen, who also took over the levying of customs duties in Braubach (until 1325). When they died out in 1479, their posses-sions went to the Landgrafen von Hessen (until 1803). The **Phi-**

Braubach: Obertor and remains of the town wall.

lippsburg at the southern entrance to the town was built by Philipp II von Hessen-Rheinfels in 1568-71 as a secondary residence. When he died, his widow used it as a place of retreat. Its «golden age» was after 1643, when Johann der Streitbare kept court here in a magnificent style. Passing through the castle gates we find ourselves in the romantic castle yard of this attractive castle.

Down beside the Rhine the visitor should not miss seeing the famous rose gardens. The tower of the Early Gothic St. Barbara's Church (14th century) was erected around 1200 and was part of the town's defences. Built-in fire-places and benches suggest that it probably used to be inhabited. The town fortifications included the Marksburg. In the town itself, the Obertor, the Pankgrafenturm and parts of the town wall are still standing. The centre of the town is full of old-world charm in which we come across picturesque corners and narrow streets with their attractive half-timbered houses.

When Napoleon reorganized the map of Germany, Braubach, which until then had been part of Hessen, went to the Duchy of Nassau in 1803, and then to Prussia in 1866. In 1900 Prussia sold the **Marksburg** for a symbolic 1000 Reichsmarks to the German Castles Association, which it still belongs today. Its excellent location on a high wooded peak made any kind of attack seemed doomed to failure. Perhaps as a result of

View of Marksburg fortress, the only Knight's castle along the Rhine still standing

this, it was never attacked or besieged in spite of its strategic position on the Rhine, and is therefore the only castle on the Rhine that dates back to Knighthood days. Barred windows bear witness to the fact that for a long time under the administration of Hessen and Nassau it was a state prison.

Walking up from Braubach or just from the large car park below the castle, we come to the first of the five gates, the drawbridge gate. In the 17th century it was reinforced by a tunnel passage, 25 m long, with mighty barrel vaults and a sharp bend in it for defence purposes. Seven guns also contributed to its defensive strenght. The outer bailey leads us on to the Fuchstor (14th century), which has a sally-gate for counter-attack purposes. Beneath the wooden bridge, which could be removed in times of danger, there was a pitfall. Crossing the inner bailey, we arrive at the embrasure gate with the castellan's tower. A staircase hewn into the rock leads beneath the Big Battery – on the Zollbachtal side – to the battery yard. An iron gate finally admits us to the triangular inner yard of the castle. In the centre of this stands the 39 m high keep. Its square 6 x 6 m base was part of the original castle built around 1200, the narrow tower was added in the 14th century. Originally it was only possible to enter it eight metres up via ladder. Prisoners were thrown into the dungeon six metres below through the «Angstloch» (Hole of Fear). Additional floors were added to the Romanesque Palas (Hall) on the north side after a fire in 1705. In the cellar, which used to be the stables, the present owner, the Castles Association, gives us an idea of mediaeval justice in the «torture chamber» containing a collection of torture and punishment instruments. To the right is the 27 m long Gothic hall with its impressive kitchen and open fire-place. Deep window recesses show how thick the curtain wall is (3 m). On the upper floor were the ladies' rooms and the 65 m² knights' hall with latrine bays in the outer wall. On the side overlooking the Rhine there is a half-timbered building put up in 1705 to replace the bakery, the well and the water-tank. This building today contains a weaving-room and an armoury – with an exhibition

Marksburg: Armoury.
Display of mediaeval
armour and weapons.

on «Armament over the Ages». The first floor of the Chapel Tower (built around 1200) is taken up by the Markuskapelle (Saint Mark's Chapel), which gave the former «Burg Braubach» its present name. In the upper bailey the present owners have planted a herb garden containing all the seasoning and medicinal herbs used in the Middle Ages among other things for witches' brews and magic potions. The castle also houses a unique library with 12,000 volumes on castles and castle history.

Marksburg: Castle kitchen in the Gothic Hall building. A whole ox on a spit could be roasted over the huge open fireplace.

The outworks «Pulvereck» and «Scharfes Eck» were added in the 17th century to reinforce the castle's defences. After 1900 the Castles Association had the whole neglected structure restored according to engravings made by the surveyor Dilich. Above the drawbridge gate – aside from the main buildings – they added a castle restaurant.
Open daily. Footpath from Braubach 25 min., from the car park 5 min.

The Königsstuhl near Rhens

Downstream from Braubach on the left bank of the Rhine lies the little town of Rhens, once situated at the meeting point of four Rhenish electors' territories. It was in an orchard here that the archbishops of Cologne, Mainz and Trier and the Elector of the Palatinate chose Rudolf von Habsburg as Emperor in 1273. The town became famous by the «Kurverein von Rhense», which agreed in 1338 that a king chosen by electors no longer needed confirmation by the Pope. It was here in Rhens that Karl IV was elected king in 1346 and Ruprecht von der Pfalz – the last one – in 1400. On the bank of the Rhine 300 m downstream, a building was erected at the end of the 14th century – the Königsstuhl.
Ruprecht's successors, elected in Frankfurt, showed themselves to the people and took their oath of allegiance here before being crowned in Aachen. The building was pulled down at the beginning of the last century but rebuilt 50 years later. The new building, now located on a hill beside the road from Rhens to Waldesch, is based on the original mediaeval one and can be considered a historic German monument.

Schloss Stolzenfels

Opposite where the River Lahn joins the Rhine and upstream from the town of Kapellen on a rocky peak stands Schloss Stolzenfels. It was built by the Archbishop of Trier Arnold von Isenburg (1242-59) only a few years after the Elector of Mainz had had Burg Lahneck put up opposite. Both castles were given the right to collect customs duties on the Rhine in the 14th century. During the unsuccessful siege of Koblenz in 1688/89 Stolzenfels was burnt to the ground by the French and left as a ruin and a quarry. The town of Koblenz gave it to Crown Prince Friedrich Wilhelm von Preussen in 1823, who had it rebuilt and extended after designs by the famous architect Schinkel. The mediaeval structure with its keep, its building overlooking the Rhine, its walls and outer bailey, remained more or less as before, but, by adding the buildings on the other side towards the hill, Schinkel created a symmetrical lay-out. The flat roofs have battlements around them like English castles. The whole construction is considered a perfect example of Rhenish Late Romanticism.
The living quarters of the King of Prussia and his wife covered both wings of the first floor. We can still admire the valuable furniture in those seven rooms, including precious antiques such as the finely crafted desk once belonging to the Elector of Trier (around 1700). A wide staircase leads us from the castle

yard through the arcades to the Mediterranean-style pergola garden with its fountain and Adjutantenturm (Adjutant's Tower) (14th century) at the far end. A gateway takes us on to the great Rhine terrace. The fountain proudly displays a Prussian eagle. The outer wall painting shows the reception of Ruprecht von der Pfalz chosen king in Rhens in 1400. Standing aside from the castle itself, the Klausengebäude (1843) with its servants' quarters, stables and coach-houses was obviously influenced in style by English Late Gothic.

Footpath 15 min. from Kapellen, a romantic serpentine pathway with a viaduct. Open 1.1. to 30.11. except Monday.

Schloss Stolzenfels: On the foundations of a knight's castle (13th century), the Crown Prince of Prussia had an English-looking castle built in Rhenish Late Romaticist style.

Burg Lahneck and Lahnstein

The area around the mouth of the River Lahn was already settled on in 4000 BC. The Electoral Mainz' **Burg Lahneck** was built in around 1240 to defend the nearby silver mines and as the northernmost bastion in the country. In the 15th century, the castle's fortifications were improved to make it able to deal with the new firearms – on each side of the old keep, a 3.5 m thick curtain wall was added. In 1688 the castle was laid in ruins by the French, then from 1852 onwards rebuilt in New Gothic style incorporating all that was left standing of the original castle. The castle con-

Burg Lahneck above Lahnstein. The keep is flanked by 3.5 m thick curtain walls on the side of attack. Opposite lies Schloss Stolzenfels, and, on the mouth of the Lahn, Niederlahnstein.

tains a delightful chapel, a Rittersaal (Knight's Hall) particularly worth seeing, as well as valuable pictures and furnitures. From the keep we are able to enjoy a magnificent panorama.

In addition to this, **Oberlahnstein** also has a second castle right beside the Rhine, built in the 14th century by Electoral Mainz as a customs fortress. The oldest part of the **Martinsburg** is its hexagonal keep. Some parts of the town fortifications are still standing, the Hexenturm (Witches' Tower) now contains a historic assembly room and a museum. In around 1160 the Romanesque Salhof was built, which is now a tourist office. In the Hochstrasse we still find a number of historic residences, but also the old Town Hall (around 1507), a Gothic half-timbered building.

Niederlahnstein: the famous «Wirtshaus an der Lahn» (1697)

Niederlahnstein, part of the town of Lahnstein since 1969, has the oldest gallery church in the middle Rhine area, the Romanesque Johanniskirche (St. John's Church), which was built from 950 onwards and redesigned with alternations added in 1130. In the Johannisstrasse we find the Märkerhof (13th century) and the Gasthaus «Schwanen» (1664). Not quite as old but all the more famous, the **«Wirtshaus an der Lahn»** (an inn beside the River Lahn) (1697) was already mentioned in Goethe's writings.

Tucked away in the park at the eastern end of the district stands the Arnsteiner Hof (16th century), which contains a dainty little Gothic chapel. A modern spa centre has been built above the urban part of Lahnstein.

Burg Lahneck open to the public April - October. Restaurant open all year round. Open-air theatre performances August/September. Castle car park. 20 minutes to walk from the bus-stop.

Oberlahnstein: Martinsburg. The Electors of Mainz had the customs fortress erected beside the Rhine in about 1300.

Koblenz and Ehrenbreitstein fortress

After the fall of the frontier fortification «Limes», the fortified Roman town of «Confluentes» became of great strategic importance as a frontier fortress. Pile bridges over the Moselle and the Rhine provided links with neighbouring regions. The Franconians replaced the ruined Roman settlement by a Royal Court (5th century). In 1018 Koblenz and the castle Ehrenbreitstein were given to the archbishops of Trier. It was here that Konrad III von Hohenstaufen was elected Emperor in 1138, and that a meeting of princes was held in 1338. In spite of the fact that Koblenz lost two-thirds of its buildings in an unsuccessful siege by Ludwig XIV's armies, the archbishops made it their residence. Under Prussian rule (from 1815 onwards) the town was turned onto a fortress, the Electoral Palace became a subsidiary residence. Today Koblenz, a city since 1962, is the home of a large garrison and has made a name for itself as a wine-growing town.

The promenades along the Rhine and the Moselle, altogether 8 km long, meet at the **«Deutsches Eck»,** a good starting-point for a walk round the **Old City**. This point where the Moselle flows into the Rhine was given its name after 1216 when the Deutschordensritter established a settlement nearby. In a charming gar-

Koblenz: Ehrenbreitstein fortress, built since 1817, as a substitute for the Electoral Trier fortress destroyed in 1799.

Koblenz: The «Plan». In the background the Baroque towers of the Liebfrauenkirche (started in the 12th century), the most striking landmark in the town's silhouette.

den park stands at the well-preserved Kompturhaus (Commander's House). The Kastor Church, consecrated in 836, is one of the most impressive Romanesque churches, and contains many works of art. In the Kastorstrasse we notice a tower with battlements, the so-called «Deutscher Kaiser». What is today the vicarage of «Our Lady» was built on the site of the Royal Court (5th century). The towers behind it are remains of the Roman town fortifications (4th century). Another Roman tower can be seen in the walls of the Gothic chancel of the Florinskirche (12th century). The buildings that stand out most along the romantic banks of the Moselle are the old castle (from the 13th century onwards), today the town library, and the stone Balduin's Bridge with its fourteen arches, built under Elector Balduin (1307-54). In the Liebfrauenkirche (Church of Our Lady) in the centre of the old town we find an unexpectedly harmonious combination of Romanesque, Gothic and Baroque architecture. Looking around, we see attractive façades, e.g. at the «Altes Kaufhaus», the «Plan», and in the Löhrstrasse. One of the town's landmarks is in the courtyard of the town hall, which used to be a Jesuit College: the Schengelbrunnen (1940) with a bronze fountain depicting a boy from Koblenz. The spacious palace near the Rhine promenade was built by Elector Clemens Wenzelslaus in 1786 in Classicist style. Near the Rhine bridge, the town had a further tourist attraction built in

Koblenz: Ornamental oriel in the pedestrian precinct.

1925, the Weindorf (Wine Village). This is an exact reproduction of a wine-growing village, giving visitors from all over the world an opportunity to enjoy the produce of German winegrowers in a romantic and typically Rhine-Moselle atmosphere.

From its 118 m high terrace opposite the mouth of the Moselle, **Ehrenbreitstein** castle and fortress has a commanding position over such a strategically important part of the Rhine valley. The first castle was built by a certain «Ehrenbert» at the end of the 10th century, a nobleman probably from the Salian-Carolingian house. From the 16th century onwards the Trier rulers had it made into a fortress, which was regarded as being invicible until about 1800. In 1688 and 1794-99, it withstood five sieges by

*The Schengelbrunnen
with a bronze fountain*

French troops. At the end of 1799, however, they managed to take the fortress by starving out the occupants, after which they demolished it with 30,000 pounds of gunpowder. The present fortress was erected from 1817 on by the Prussians in Classicist style. Rounded archways with carefully finished openings, capitals, blind arcades and accentuated horizontal joints contrast with the simple, monumental façade of this functional building. Once a year the fortress and the town of Koblenz are illuminated with Bengal lights as part of the great firework display **«Rhein in Flammen»** (The Rhine on Fire).
Car parks near the fortress _ Chair-lift.

Koblenz: Deutsches Eck. The spit of land where the Moselle and Rhine meet got its name from the Deutschordensritter (Knights) who settled nearby in 1216.

Vallendar

Towered over by a majestically high building, the old wine-growing town of Vallendar is located approximately 3 kilometres downriver from the Ehrenbreitstein fortress. The Meffert House and the graceful building "Auf'm Nippes", both originating from around 1700, stand out among the trim half-timbered houses in the lanes of the old town centre. While travelling along the Rhine, Goethe was a frequent guest in the magnificent Baroque palace built by the D'Ester family on the foundation walls of the former citadel.

A short way from the town centre there are the architecturally interesting buildings of the apostolic "Beautiful Town Movement" clustered in a group around their place of pilgrimage, the chapel of a former **Augustinian Convent** (12th century). The Niederwerth, which is also a part of the town, is the only inhabited island on the Rhine.

Bendorf and its Suburb Sayn

The extensive industrial town of Bendorf – also on the right bank of the river – includes the suburb of Sayn on its eastern fringes. On a rocky projection from the mountainside there is the ruin of a castle which has been in the possession of the Grafen (Counts) von Sayn since the 10th century, albeit with the occasional interruption, and which now has the 19th generation of owners from this family. Whereas three sides of this castle could make use of natural protection provided by the steep slopes in which it was embedded, the owners had a moat dug out in the direction of the mountain, additionally safeguarded by a mighty battlemented parapet with sentry walk. The walls of the 20 metre high castle keep (12th century) are 2.40 metres thick. A Gothic sectional wall is connected to these. A 20 metre wide and 90 metre long outer bailey on the side remains to a large extent preserved up to the present day. On the two lower storeys of the castle keep there is the **Turmuhrenmuseum** (Tower Clock Museum) with 25 exhibits gathered from 5 centuries. It is from the museum that the visitor can reach the western sentry walk of the battlements and a platform affording a view over the surrounding

Sayn Abbey: Reliquary of Saint Simon (around 1220)

Bendorf-Sayn: The ruin of the Neogothic castle with the restored castle tower. Beyond the ruins of the citadel living quarters and the citadel.

countryside. Nowadays the castle grounds accomodate a game park, the castle refectory (licensed) offers refreshments for the tired visitor.

In the 15th century the Counts had the middle castle residence built below the main castle for a daughter to live in. Further down the slope we can see the remains of **Burg Stein** (Stein Castle), the ruins of which were sold by the famous Baron von und zum Stein in 1802. Another castle residence was built at the foot of the mountain by the Lords von Reiffenberg in the 15th century. In 1757 their heirs transformed it into a Baroque castle, and it finally came into the possession of Count Ludwig von Sayn-Wittgenstein-Sayn in 1848. The Count added to the original building and had it converted into a magnificent Neogothic residence. The castle was damaged in the Second World War and has fallen into decay since this time. The far-ranging castle park, however, still induces the visitor to take a long, enjoyable walk.

One monument is in remembrance of Emperor Wilhelm I, who often stayed here as the guest of Count Ludwig. But the main attraction of the grounds today is a newly laid out dream landscape with lakes, splendid plants and blossoms as well as gorgeous indigenous and tropical butterflies.

The three gun barrels on the castle square remind us of the Sayn ironworks, which were in production from 1769 to 1926. The period after 1815, when this area was conquered by the Prussians, brought a boom to the iron production here. Apart from outstanding examples of wrought cast iron – which can be admired in the

Stadtmuseum Bendorf (Bendorf Town Museum) – the ironworks produced heavy artillery and ammunition for the nearby fortresses of Koblenz and Ehrenbreitstein. In 1830 the building of the impressive former foundry hall was started, using cast iron and glass and constructed on the model of Gothic cathedrals. This industrial monument, one of the most significant in Europe, can still be visited nowadays in the Sayntal (Sayn Valley).

The Brexbachtal (Brexbach Valley) runs along the east side of the mountain on the slopes of which the castle is located. Below the old fortress we can see Heins Mühle (Heins Mill), constructed in the 19th century and a building of significant interest in history and technology. Lovingly restored, it serves nowadays as a mill museum. Somewhat further along the banks of the stream there is the former **Prämonstratenserabtei** (Premonstratensian Abbey), founded by Count Heinrich III and his brothers around 1200. It was at the same time that the single-nave Abbey Church was built, 60 metres long and a mere 7.7 metres wide. The tower was renovated in the 18th century. Only a few of the precious decorative pieces escaped falling victim to the vicissitudes of the turbulent Lutheran Reformation, for example the baptismal font (around 1220), the gilded shrine with the arm relic of Saint Simon and other relics.

However, the many tombs of abbots and aristocratic benefactors from the 13th to the 18th centuries, the west wing of the cloisters as well as the Abbey with its impressive roofed well (around 1230) are worth a visit.

Neuwied

To the west of Bendorf the right bank of the Rhine retreats to give rise to the Neuwieder Becken (Neuwied Basin). It is protected by a 7.5 kilometre long flood-dyke which is unique along the Rhine.

Neuwied Castle, formerly a hunting lodge and country seat of the Archbishops of Trier

The suburb of **Engers** near the mouth of the Saynbach (Sayn stream) was fortified by a Roman watchtower as early as in the 4th century. In 1758 the Archbishop of Trier, J. Ph. von Walderdorff, had the old Burg Kunostein (Kunostein Castle) demolished and commissioned a pupil of the famous Baroque artist Balthasar Neumann to erect a hunting lodge and country seat in its place. This is still in good repair today. Of special interest is the splendid banqueting hall, decorated with precious ornaments as well as wall paintings and painted ceilings in the Rococo style. In the close vicinity of the lodge we can find the picturesque market square with its stylish town hall (1642) and the lodge inn.

The Raiffeisen Bridge between Neuwied and Weißenturm.

Some distance away from the river there is the suburb of **Heimbach-Weis**. The former Prämonstratenserkloster (Premonstratensian Monastery) (12th to 18th centuries) contains a wealth of instructive material on the history of architecture, showing as it does objects embodying the Romantic, the Gothic and the Baroque styles. On the outskirts of the forest the municipality has established a zoo which is in its setting and landscaping the most charming in the Middle Rhine area, letting the visitor enjoy not only the animals but also a splendid far-reaching view into the Rhine Valley and over the mountains of the Eifel. From this point well tended footpaths cross the recreational area and follow the Roman Limes with its reconstructed watchtower and former fortress up to a long way inside the Rhine-Westerwald nature park.

At the point where the Wied stream forms a small knoll which it passes just before flowing into the plain, the Lords of Wied built a castle around 1100 in what is now the suburb of **Altwied**. This castle fell into disrepair after the Counts had transferred their residence to the Rhine in 1653. Beneath the ruins the visitor can find picturesque nooks and crannies.

Passing through the suburb of **Segendorf** we reach Monrepos, a viewpoint offering panoramic scenery. The "Museum des Eiszeitalters" (Museum of the Ice-Age), a department of the Roman-Germanic Museum, is located in this magnificent landscape. It presents discoveries from the earliest prehistory of the Rhineland.

The Castle of the Wied princes was built in the 17th century near to the Wied estuary and is nowadays the **"Schloßtheater"** (Castle Theatre). It was also at this time that Neuwied was founded, today the centre of a flourishing community with 65,000 inhabitants. Near the suburb of Feldkirchen – with its historical "Feldkirche" (church) – the mountain slopes of the Westerwald approach the Rhine again.

The modern Raiffeisen-Brücke (Raiffeisen Bridge) is the link between Neuwied and the **Weißenthurm** (White Tower) on the opposite bank, which takes its name from a toll tower in the 14th century.

Andernach

Andernach, the "baker's apprentice town" is located on the left side of the Rhine on the site of an ancient settlement. Excavation finds have proved that people lived here as early as 400,000 years ago. Around the beginning of the new era the Romans established

their fort under the name of "Antunnacum", and the town formed the southern cornerstone of the electoral prinicipality of Cologne between 1167 and appoximately 1800. It is then hardly surprising that in this capacity the town was often the object of hard fighting, but the remains of the town walls (12th century) with their gates and towers bear witness to its powers of defence.

Andernach: The Round Tower (1440–1452), 56 metres high, was the most mighty construction in the town fortifications.

Of particular interest in this regard are the 56 metre high "Runder Turm" (Round Tower), built in the 15th century, which even withstood an attack with explosives by the French troops in 1689, the ruins of the town castle as well as the Koblenzer Tor (Koblenz Gate) and the Rheintor (Rhine Gate). This is the legendary location of the heroic defence put up by the bakers' apprentices, who, although greatly outnumbered, are said to have driven off the enemy forces by throwing beehives. A monument in the inner courtyard of the bastion (12th to 13th centuries) was erected in remembrance of this legend. The well tended grounds on the bank offer visitors many rare botanical specimens as well as the Old Crane (1554–1559), a technical masterpiece of its time. It was used for loading millstones up to 1911.

Andernach: Ruin of the town fortress castle (12th century)

Andernach: View across the well-tended Rhine banks to the mediaeval "Rheintor" (Rhine Gate).

A stroll through the old city gives visitors many opportunities of insight into Andernach's turbulent past.

The **"Altes Rathaus"** (Old Town Hall) was mentioned as early as 1407, a time when it was still being used as a synagogue by the Jewish community. A staircase leads down underneath the council chamber to the former bathing room.

In the 16th to 18th centuries the provostry of the **Himmerod** Monastery was located in the nearby "Himmeroder Hof". The Romanesque **"Mariendom"** (Cathedral of the Virgin Mary), built on the foundation walls of an older church around 1200, is distinguished by the harmonious structure of the chevet. The **"Christuskirche"** (Christchurch) (1245–1450), nowadays a protestant place of worship, originally belonged to the **"Minoritenkloster"** (Minorite Monastery). It has only one side nave and in former centuries used to be the favoured burial place of the Rhineland aristocracy.

Andernach offers its visitors a great variety of leisure facilities and is a convenient point of departure for excursions to the "Laacher See" (Laach Lake) with the remarkable **"Benediktiner-Abtei Maria-Laach"** (Benedictine Abbey of Maria-Laach) (around 1200), to the famous Nürburgring with its motor-races and the racing sports museum, as well as to the suburb of Namedy with its charming lake castle, a former citadel from the 16th century, and its mediaeval church. The Rhine island "Namedyer Werth" offered an attraction of a very special kind in past years: at regular intervals a fountain of mineral water spurted out of the earth up to 60 metres high like a geyser. The water, coming from a depth of more than 300 metres, is used today in the beverage industry.

The Maria-Laach Benedictine Abbey (around 1200) is well worth making an excursion into the countryside of the middle Rhine Valley.

Leutesdorf

The vineyards of this most famous wine-growing village on the middle Rhine cover kilometres of the riverbanks opposite the Rhine island. Leutesdorf, the merry wine centre at the end of the Neuwied Basin, with only 2,000 inhabitants, has more than 1 million vines. Visitors can enjoy not only the precious juice of the grape but also a restful and relaxing time without any of the nuisances of industrial living. However, this romantic wine-growing village also has several monuments which are well worth seeing: beautiful former court demesnes and half-timbered houses in narrow lanes and along the banks of the Rhine, the ruins of the old town fortifications, the **"Pfarrkirche"** (Parish Church), the building of which was started in the 13th century, with its wall paintings, as well as the **"Wallfahrtskirche Heiligkreuz"** (Pilgrims' Church of the Holy Cross), which is still visited by devout pilgrims and is decorated with beautiful Baroque altars.

Hammerstein

Where the Rhine Valley closes to its narrowest point between the Westerwald and the Eifel we can find the sister communities of Oberhammerstein and Niederhammerstein nestling on the right banks of the river. The steep vineyards provide the grapes for a full-bodied, rich wine. The bells of the Romanesque parish church (11th century) are said to have been cast around 1050.
This would make them the oldest church bells in the middle Rhine area. A further attraction is the **"Burgmannshof"** (16th century). Before the turn of the millenium the ancient "Burg Hammerstein" (Hammerstein Castle), built on steep grey wacke rock, guarded the

The "Burgmannshof" in Oberhammerstein dates back to the 16th century.

village of the same name. After it had been forced to capitulate from threatening starvation by Heinrich II at the beginning of the 11th century, it continued its existence as a "Reichsburg" (Imperial Castle). Emperor Heinrich IV had the fortress renovated and it was here that he found a place of refuge and defence for himself and the Imperial Crown Jewels against his son Heinrich V in 1105. In the 14th century the village was granted municipal rights, and the burgraves received the entitlement of the "Kleine Münze" (small coin), the castle was given to the electoral Trier as a fief.

Rheinbrohl

The greatest Roman construction north of the Alps, the **Limes**, began directly adjacent to the outskirts of the village. Erected in the first three centuries AD, it formed a link betwen the Middle Rhine and the Danube and shielded the Roman provinces from attacks by Germanic tribes. Watchtowers, originally made of wood and then rebuilt of stone, were set up in sight of each other, connected by 2.5 metre high palisades behind which a 3 metre trench was dug out. Behind this line many military camps were established for the legionaries. The first of these citadels was near Rheinbrohl, the first watchtower in the forest towards Bad Hönningen has been reconstructed. From this point visitors interested in the history of the Romans in Germany can take a walk following the course of the Limes.

Burg Rheineck

On the opposite bank of the Rhine, on a wooded hilltop between Brohl and Bad Breisig, there towers the old "Pfalzgrafenburg" (Count Palatinate Castle). After it had been destroyed by King Konrad III in 1151, it became the property of the Archbishopric of Cologne. The new owners rebuilt their fortress, a task which became necessary again after the second destruction (1282, Rudolf von Habsburg). When the castle was again ravaged in 1689, it was built entirely anew in 1832. Only the massive **"Bergfried"** (castle keep) from the 11th century and the Romanesque castle chapel have remained as witnesses to the original mediaeval edifice.

"Burg Rheineck" (Rheineck Castle) above Bad Breisig was constructed in 1832 from the ruins of a Palatine Count's castle built in the 11th century.

Bad Breisig

For more than 900 years the tiny country of Breisig belonged to the Bishopric of Essen, before Napoleon expropriated the possessions of the church by decree of the Imperial Deputation. The suburb of Oberbreisig still has a mediaeval church dating from the 13th century.

Today there are still three thermal spas flowing in Niederbreisig. One of them is the "Mariensprudel", which provides the open-air thermal swimming pool with water of 28 degrees centigrade. The "Geiersprudel" is even better known – its carbonic water, with a temperature of 32 degrees centigrade, supplies the spa house named after it as well as an indoor thermal swimming pool. The spa house of the "Ludgerussprudel" is in the well-tended spa park, whereas the "Gertrudisquelle" (15 degrees centigrade) is the source for the open-air mineral pool.

Bad Niederbreisig: Parade of attractive half- timbered houses leading down to the Rhine.

Visitors will see all around them the attractive residences of the 17th and 18th centuries. The town also offers a riverside walkway of 6 kilometres, a varied and interesting entertainment programme for spa guests, a large number of walking and leisure facilities as well as festivities during which visitors can have first-hand experience of the proverbial gaiety of the inhabitants of the Rhineland.

Bad Hönningen

From the Rhine walkway in Niederbreisig we can look over the river directly to the Bad Hönningen riverside walk. This town is the head-quarters of the community association which also includes Leutesdorf, Rheinbrohl and Hammerstein. Bad Hönningen also has thermal spas, which supply the water for (among other facilities) a combined open-air and indoor swimming pool complex, heating it to a temperature of between 26 and 36 degrees centigrade. Directly adjacent to this swimming-pool complex and forming a part of it is a large rest-cure meadow on the Rhine, which for its part borders onto a camping site. An inviting spa park and the modern pedestrian pre-cinct with numerous street cafes, restaurants and shops tempt the visitor to take an enjoyable stroll. Anyone wanting to go in for more serious walking can make full use of the possibilities offered by the vineyards and the adjacent nature park, with over 60 kilometres of marked paths. Like most of the other villages and towns in the Rhineland, Bad Hönningen's calendar of yearly events would not be

Bad Hönningen: The spa gardens and the extensive Rhine river-side grounds invite visitors to take a quiet stroll.

complete without the celebration of festivities: apart from Carneval, visitors can enjoy events such as hop-gathering, vine-blossoms, summer night and "Federweißer" (new wine) festivities.
Located on a flat-topped hill amidst vineyards, "Schloß Arenfels" (Arenfels Castle) catches the eye of visitors travelling along the Rhine. Because of its strategically unfavourable location the owners of the old citadel (around 1260) had it reconstructed as a castle with beautiful parks at the end of the Middle Ages.

*Bad
Hönningen:
Arenfels Castle*

*Linz: The old
town hall, built
in 1392 ▶*

Linz

Before we reach Linz we first come to the suburb of **Leubsdorf**, a charming wine-growing village with trim halftimbered houses. The first mention of this village is in an original document dating back to the 7th century and recording the gift from Pippin I to his daughter Gertrud, the abbess of the Convent of Nivelles in Belgium. For this reason the location still goes under the name of "Gertrude Vineyard". The slopes above the gardens on the banks of the Rhine give a splendid view over the mouth of the Ahr.
Exactly opposite Leubsdorf we see Linz, the "colourful town on the Rhine", one of the most frequently visited places in the region.

Linz: View to the Parish Church of Leubsdorf.

Dreamy nooks and crannies and streets with coloured half-timbered houses have helped to make the ancient town famous. Having been granted municipal rights in 1320, Linz built the fortified walls and town towers of local basalt. Of the original fortifications there still remain the main entrances, the "Neutor" (New Gate) and the "Rheintor" (Rhine Gate). The axial street between the two is called "Mittelstraße" (Middle Street). Nowadays this is a pedestrian precinct with benches, seats and many inns and restaurants where visitors may enjoy staying a while. The white paving reminds us that a stream once flowed here and likewise at the Butter Market. Here we can see an original statue of "Agnes", the market woman, who used to sell eggs, cheese and butter.

The **"Rathausplatz"** (Town Hall Square) with the "Mariensäule" (Column of the Virgin Mary) is the centre of the old town. Here stands the oldest town hall in the Rhineland-Palatinate, built in 1392. Three times a day various melodies are played by its 23-piece chiming bells. The remarkable town hall clock was installed in 1737.

The old and new half-timbered houses around the "Neutor" (New Gate) form a splendid scene. In front of them there stands the bronze statue of the **"Klapperjunge"** (rattle boy). According to ancient tradition the "church bells fly" to Rome on Good Friday and Easter Saturday. Every year on these two days about 200 children as "rattle boys" make up for the missing sound of the bells by walking in procession through the streets of the old town with wooden rattles at 6 am, midday and 6 pm to announce the time of day.

The opposite end of the street used to be protected by the "Rheintor" (Rhine Gate), which, together with three splendid gabled houses and the castle, transform the castle square into a magnificent theatrical backdrop.

When in 1365 one of the 11 toll points for shipping between Cologne and Mainz was established in Linz, the Archbishopric of Cologne began simultaneously with the construction of the fortified toll-collecting castle. This castle carried out its tasks up to the beginning of the 19th century, when toll duties on the Rhine were abol-

Linz: Former fortified toll-collecting castle

ished. Present-day visitors can still visit the "Angstloch" (pit of fear), the dungeon with a torture chamber and instruments bearing witness to the inhuman interrogation methods of past centuries. The buildings also accomodate a restaurant, the **"Klingendes Museum"** (Museum of Sound) with self-playing mechanical musical instruments as well as a castle discotheque. The venerable **"St.-Martins-Kirche"** (St. Martin's Church), consecrated in 1214, possesses late-Romanesque frescoes which are of great significance in the history of art. A famous tripartite altar-piece, once belonging to the "Marienaltar" (Altar of Our Lady)in this church, has in the meantime been erected in the "Pfarrkirche St. Marien" (St. Mary's Parish Church).

Linz offers not only historical attractions but also leisure facilities for every taste. Of the numerous possibilities let us mention only the open-air swimming pool, the paths for strolls along the banks of the Rhine, walks in the nearby nature park as well as many festivities.

Linz: The Castle Square with the "Rheintor" (Rhine Gate)

Sinzig

The old town of Sinzig is located near to the mouth of the Ahr, a small distance from the river on the middle Rhine terrace. Even before the arrival of the Romans there was a Celtic settlement here on fertile arable land. There is evidence that a Franconian Royal Palatinate existed here from 762 – before the time of Charlemagne. For as long as up to 1531 most German kings broke their journey here on their way to the coronation in Aachen. Especially the Staufer dynasty was smitten by the charms of the **"Sinziger Reich"** (Sinzig Realm): Emperor Friedrich Barbarossa alone stayed here four times. The old fortification ring was established under the rule of his successors, who had courts and aristocratic residences built in the town by their vassals and in the surrounding countryside by their knights so as to protect the royal route to Aachen.

The founding of the **"Peterskirche"**, (St. Peter's Church), built by the Aachen tithe court in 1225, can also be traced back to Staufer influence. This church is considered to be a classic example of the transition from the Romanesque
to the Gothic styles of architecture; the facade is ornamented and it has an impressively spacious effect in the interior. With the erection of the nearby **"Stauferburg Landskron"** castle in 1206 Sinzig lost its position of major importance, but it remained a centre of viniculture and became a significant stopping place for pilgrims.

Not only the "Peterskirche" (St. Peter's Church) calls to mind the former importance of the town – the mediaeval tithe court, the remains of the town walls and the Sinzig Castle also bear witness to this time.

It was built in 1336 as the fortified domicile of the Margrave of Jülich, enlarged and converted into a castle in the 16th century and destroyed in 1688. In the middle of the last century it arose again as a Neogothic manor for a wealthy merchant. The elements remaining from the former construction are the wide moat, the lower part of the north-eastern tower and an adjacent wall.

*Sinzig Castle with
Folk Museum*

Remagen

The suburb of Kripp to the north of the mouth of the Ahr marks the beginning of the outskirts of the town of Remagen, the most northern town on the Rhine to be part of the Rhineland-Palatinate. Originally a Celtic settlement, it was a Roman garrison town for almost 400 years, after which, however, it rapidly lost significance. It was seized in pledge several times and was a centre for craftsmen and small wine-growers. The building of the "Apollinariskirche" (Apollinaris Church) (1839–1842) in the vicinity brought an incredible boom to the town : members of European princely families visited the wonderful edifice and large hotels were established along Remagen's Rhine banks. At about the same time the Cologne-Düsseldorf steamship company built a Rhine shipyard and a pier at Remagen. The town finally became the undisputed centre of the tourist trade after the extension of the railway-line network on the Rhine and through the Ahr Valley.

It was in the last year of the Second World War that Remagen took its place in the annals of history : after two attempts made by German pioneers to blow up the bridge at Remagen had failed, Allied troups marched across the bridge on 7th March 1945, thus crossing the Rhine for the first time. Exactly ten days later this bridge, built in 1916–1918, collapsed for no apparent reason, sweeping American

Towers of the Bridge of Remagen

pioneers, who were busy repairing the substance, into the river. The bridge towers on either side of the Rhine bear witness to that memorable time, in particular the tower on the Remagen bank with the collection of exhibits in the **"Friedensmuseum Brücke von Remagen"** (Bridge of Remagen Peace Museum). This museum contains a collec-

Remagen: The Market Square with the Town Hall.

tion of material on the history of the former Ludendorff Bridge as well as on the holders of the Nobel Peace Prize from all over the world. A memorial chapel – near to the attractive all-season swimming pool – is dedicated to the German soldiers in the then prisoner-of-war camp named **"Goldene Meile"** (Golden Mile). This chapel takes its name from the **"Schwarze Madonna"** (Black Madonna), sculpted by prisoners in the camp. The Gothic chapel (15th century) in the centre of the town is now a **Roman Museum**. Very near to the museum there is the parsonage with the fountain of the Virgin Mary. Behind this a part of the mediaeval town walls is preserved. If we walk through the aperture in the wall at this point, we can see the mysterious Romanesque parish gate (12th century) portraying the 8 capital sins.

In the reconstruction of the **"Pfarrkirche St. Peter und Paul"** (Parish Church of St. Peter and St. Paul) the architects were outstandingly successful in integrating the old house of God (1264) harmoniously into the new church. The main attractions here are the excellent Gothic paintings as well as the late Gothic tabernacle which dates back to 1500, as does the choir vault.

The unmistakable silhouette of the **"Apollinariskirche"** (Apollinaris Church) stands out against the sky on a hilltop near Remagen. In the 12th century the provostry and a Benedictine church were built here on the site of a former Martins chapel. Around 1530 the mortal remains of the saint and martyr Apollinaris were brought to the church, which since this time has been visited by large numbers of pilgrims.

After the dissolution of the monastery (1802) the Princes of Fürstenberg-Stammheim gained possession of the property, which has been a burial place for the members of their family ever since.

It was also at this time that Count Franz-Egon commissioned Zwirner, the master builder of cathedrals from Cologne, with the construction of the present-day church in place of the dilapidated old building. The four towers of the Neogothic edifice point to the four cardinal points of the compass. The two long windows on the south wall and the west wall ensure great natural illumination of the wall surfaces with the elaborate frescoes of the Nazarenes.

This group of artists from the Düsseldorf school championed a renewal of religious painting and provided the Apollinaris Church with a harmonious set of artistic portrayals in a simple style. The frescoes were finished in 1857 and in the same year the relic — the head of Saint Apollinaris — was brought into the church, which was entrusted by the Count's family to the care of the Franciscans, who have attended to the holding of services and the welfare of the pilgrims ever since. Great numbers of pious pilgrims throng over the stations of the Cross from the Rhine to the mountain especially on 25th January, the anniversary of the conveyance of the relic, and in the weeks following 22nd July, the name day of the saint.

During these eight days of celebration the relic is displayed in the church for worship. At other times it rests in a stone sarcophagus in the crypt, built in the Byzantine style.

The Apollinaris Church (1839–1842) near Remagen with its graceful towers is reminiscent of Cologne Cathedral.

Erpel and Unkel

The Ludendorff Bridge used to lead across the Rhine from Remagen to the tranquil village of Erpel. Large residencesfrom the Baroque era, mainly set in extensive gardens as befits the style of this time, look out over the Rhine.The houses in the lanes are predominantly half-timbered buildings. A graceful fountain column (1753) stands under a 100 year old plane tree on the picturesque market square.

The Baroque town hall with its delicate ridge turret is only a little more recent than the fountain. The church square is dominated by a 250 year old copper-beech. The bells of the **St. Severinus** parish church date from the 14th to the 18th centuries. Remains of the town walls with the "Neutor" (New Gate), built in the 14th century, and the soccage arch remind us of less peaceful times for the citizens on the Rhine. And yet many idyllic places from these days have been

View across the Rhine to the old wine-growing village of Unkel with its early Gothic parish church.

preserved, such as the hectagonal garden house near the former soccage court.

A stroll past free-standing houses set in elevated gardens to the "Erpeler Ley", a 200 metre high basalt rock, rewards us with a magnificent view over the Eifel, the Westerwald and the Rhine.

The wine-growing village of Erpel is located at a point where the Rhine Valley widens out. It has one of the most beautiful riverside walks on the Rhine, on which no motorised traffic is allowed. Picturesque half-timbered houses in romantic lanes and remains of the former town walls have an antique charm. Visitors can admire the rich decoration of the early Gothic parish church. Those interested in walking tours will find a variety of opportunities in a well tended network of paths through vineyards and the forests of the Siebengebirge mountain range and of the Westerwald.

The legendary Roland's Arch is all that remains of a mediaeval castle belonging to the Archbishops of Cologne.

Rolandseck

Towering over the villa suburb of Remagen on the left river bank there is the legendary "Rolandsbogen" (Roland's arch) on a hill 105 metres above the Rhine. It is all that remains of a mediaeval castle (around 1100), which used to be the toll citadel of the Archbishops of Cologne.

When the bow of the former window crashed down in 1840, its reconstruction was financed by donations from all over the world. The famous legend of the Roland's arch might also date back to this time: Knight Roland accompanied Emperor Charlemagne to Spain on a crusade against the Saracenes and fought very bravely. A short time later the false message reached his home town that he had fallen in battle. On hearing this, Hildegund, his bride, the daughter of the "Ritter vom Drachenfels" (Knight of the Dragon Rock) renounced worldly life and went into a convent on the **"Rheininsel Nonnenwerth"** (Rhine Island of Nonnenwerth), only a short distance downstream from the "Rolandseck". Now it was Roland's turn to be deeply distressed when, upon his return, he learnt what had happened. He withdrew into his castle, which he had built for his beloved bride, and looked out of the bow window across to the convent every day. A few years later Hildegund died and shortly afterwards Roland was also found dead, still staring out of the window.

From the ivy-covered arch and the restaurant we can enjoy a splendid view over to the Siebengebirge, to Bad Honnef and to the Rhine with the islands of Grafenwerth and Nonnenwerth (with the former Franciscan convent).

Nature-lovers can find above the town an impressive game park in which the animals pass by on the extensive grounds almost as in their natural surroundings.

From its partially unwooded summit in clear weather there is a magnificent view all around the world-famous panorama showing the Rhine and the Siebengebirge. Also to be recommended is an excursion to the Rodderberg (195 metres) nature preserve located to the west of Rolandswerth.

Bad Honnef with Rhöndorf

With its location protected from the elements by the Siebengebirge, Bad Honnef has a mild climate with balanced temperatures. Here, in the "German Nice", plants blossom one to two weeks earlier than in other parts of the Rhine Valley. One of the most regular spa visitors was Queen Sophia of Sweden, who stayed here a total of ten times, in each case for several months. The visitor can enjoy charming walks through the spa park and through the town across one of the bridges to the traffic-free island of Grafenwert with its ancient giant trees, extensive lawns and recreation grounds on the banks. A host of grassy areas, gardens and fountains bordering the lanes give the whole town the appearance of one large garden. The town also offers many facilities for sports and leisure activities, is famous for its schools and educational institutions, as a centre for conferences and congresses.

The slopes above the town centre are the location for the historical and traditional suburbs with their charming half-timbered houses behind which there are the endless forests of the Siebengebirge. The suburb of Rhöndorf became the most famous as the former place of residence of **Konrad Adenauer**, the first Federal German Chancellor. Here we can see his house, nowadays the **Adenauermuseum** as well as his last place of rest.

Königswinter

While the suburbs of Bonn on the left bank of the Rhine present a compact built-up area, the right bank is towered over by the volcanic hilltops of the Siebengebirge, the "Rhine Alps". Stones were quarried from the mountains as early as the Middle Ages and were used, for example, for the building of Cologne Cathedral. In the 18th and 19th centuries quarrying for trachyte, which was in great demand, was carried out in such an irresponsible way that parts of the **"Burg Drachenfels"** (Dragon Rock Castle) collapsed: the castle chapel and

The "Drachenfels" with citadel and castle ▲

◀ Drachenburg Castle

Drachenfels ruin ▼

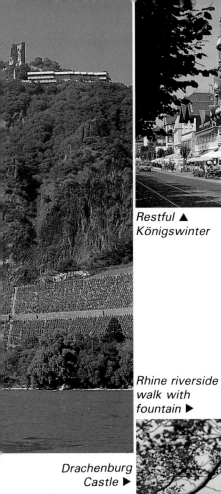

Restful ▲
Königswinter

Rhine riverside
walk with
fountain ▶

Drachenburg
Castle ▶

▼ Cog railway

the outer works of the castle in 1800, for example. However, the abuse was not stopped until the Prussian Government acquired possession of the Drachenfels hilltop in 1836 and, shortly afterwards, decreed the preservation of the foliage trees. Two interest groups, the "Association for Saving the Siebengebirge" and the "Association for the Protection of the Beauty of the Siebengebirge" championed the cause of this beautiful area, which in 1922 finally became the first German nature preserve and in 1959 the first nature park in North Rhine-Westfalia. In the meantime it has even been honoured by the award of the "European Diploma". Nowadays it serves the densely populated urban areas around Cologne and Bonn as an easily accessible weekend recreation area.

At the foot of this mountain range there is the picturesque town of Königswinter amidst the most northern self-contained vinicultural area in Germany. The visitor can walk through winding Rhine lanes to old churches and chapels or to the remarkable **"Siebengebirgsmuseum"**.

Numerous facilities for leisure activities round off the varied entertainment programme offered. However, the main attraction of the town is the world-famous **Drachenfels** with its legendary **Drachenburg** : it is here that the dragon of the Siegfried legend is said to have dwelled.

The oldest **"Zahnradbahn"** (cog railway) in Germany, dating back to 1883, brings throngs of tourists to the top of the mountain, while others prefer to travel by horse-drawn carriage, on donkey-back or even "on Shanks's pony".

From the summit, 321 metres above sea-level, we can enjoy a magnificent panorama allowing views as far as the German capital of Bonn and the volcanic mountains of the Eifel.

Impressive remains of the castle keep of this former electoral Cologne castle (12th century) are still preserved, despite it having been occupied several times by Spain and Sweden during the 30 year war and razed to the ground in 1634.

Halfway up the slope of the "Drachenfels" the "Drachenburg" (1879–1885) was built, one of the last castles to be constructed on the Rhine. A small zoo has been set up in the nearby "Nibelungenhalle" with a crocodile farm and a snake farm. This zoo has one of the largest collections of crocodiles in Europe as well as an open-air preserve unique in Germany for crocodiles, the relatives of the legendary dragon.

The impressive remains of a **"Zisterzienserabteikirche"** (Cistercian Abbey Church) dating back to the 19th century can be visited in the suburb of Heisterbach. In the vicinity of this there is the Weilberg Nature Monument, a natural picture book on the development of a volcanic landscape.

Bonn

Opposite Königswinter there is the row of picturesque villages with the names Mehlem, Muffendorf, Rüngsdorf and Plittersdorf, nowadays a part of Bad Godesberg, the most famous suburb of Bonn. Here on the Rhine, mostly with a view over the Siebengebirge, numerous diplomatic corps have established their headquarters. Their residences are mainly surrounded by large parks. These, together with the Redoute Park and the Municipal Park, at the same time a spa garden, form the "green lung" of the spacious spa of Bad Godesberg. Nature lovers will be delighted by the unusual species of trees. On the outskirts of the two adjacent public parks there is the former ballroom hall of the electoral princes, the **Redoute** (1790–1792) as well as the **"Kunstmuseum"** (Museum of Art), the former court theatre of the electoral princes.

The **Godesburg** on its basalt summit towers majestically over the suburb. This castle was built in 1210 as a defence for the Archbishopric of Cologne and was destroyed in 1583. The mighty keep, 32 metres high, offers an inspiring panorama. A hotel and restaurant were constructed on the location of the remains of the for-

Bonn-Bad Godesberg: Most famous suburb of Bonn with the ruin of the Godesburg.

tress in 1961. The **"Michaelskapelle"** (St. Michael's Chapel), a much older building located at the foot of the mountain, was decorated in the 17th century with baroque stucco ornaments. On the right bank of the Rhine Oberkassel, the first suburb of Bonn, is immediately adjacent to Königswinter.

Although it is an industrial location, Oberkassel still has a traditional town centre with beautiful half-timbered houses dating back to the

Bonn: The former castle residence of the Electoral Princes and Archbishops of Cologne – now the university building.

17th century and the renowned Schaumburger Hof, the scene of many historical events.

In 1989 Bonn celebrated its 2000th anniversary and also the 40th anniversary of its becoming the capital city of the Federal Republic of Germany. A thriving community developed from the even older Celtic settlement and the Roman camp around the beginning of the new era. During the late baroque period it was here that the electoral princes of Cologne built their **"Residenzschloß"** (Residence) (1725), which is the present-day university building. The "Rathaus" (Town Hall) and the "Koblenzer Tor" (Koblenz Gate) date back to about the same time.

The father and grandfather of the famous composer **Ludwig van Beethoven** were musicians at the court of the electoral prince. Beethoven's birthplace in the Bonngasse is still furnished as it was during the great composer's life and is nowadays a museum. Among

Bonn: late Baroque town hall (18th century)

many other exhibits bearing witness to the time of Beethoven, we can see the keyboard of the organ on which he played as a young man in the then **"Minoritenkirche"** (Minorite Church). This high Gothic basilica with its three naves (1274–1317) served the Minorite Order as a church. Since the dissolution of the monastery in 1806 it has borne the name "Remigius Church". The **"Münster-Basilika"** (Minster Basilica) (12th/13th centuries), built on a Roman burial place, is even older and more famous. In 1314 and 1346 coronations were held here.

The edifice is particularly impressive on account of its 92 metre high, sturdy lantern tower and the Romanesque cloister.

Bonn: View to the modern opera house

Bonn: Beethoven monument

The "Alter Friedhof" (Old Cemetery) to the west of the cathedral square is also a jewel. It is the last resting place for many famous people including the literary historian A. W. von Schlegel, the critical poet E. M. Arndt, the mother of Beethoven and the wife of Friedrich Schiller, Robert and Clara Schumann as well as Mildred Scheel.

The suburb of Poppelsdorf is located to the south-west of the centre of Bonn. The spacious and leafy Poppelsdorfer Allee leads to the **"Schloß Clemensruhe"** (Clemensruhe Castle), built between 1715 and 1730. Its extensive park, half of which is surrounded by a small lake, is now kept as a botanic garden. If we continue in the same direction we reach the "Kreuzberg" (125 metres above sea-level) with its **"Franziskanerkloster"** (Franciscan Monastery). The baroque church of this monastery (1627/1628) was robbed of its treasures in 1689. After its restoration it became world-renowned for the added construction of the "Scala Sancta" (sacred steps) (1746–1751), a masterpiece created by Balthasar Neumann.

Near to the Konrad Adenauer Bridge on both sides of the Rhine is the extensive Rheinaue leisure park with its many lakes and streams. Beyond this the "Langer Eugen", the lower parliamentary house of the Federal German Government, marks the location of the governmental district. Here the many residences of the representatives of various countries stand in large numbers between the parliamentary building, the offices of the German chancellor, the press building and the German federal press offices. Whereas the **Villa Hammerschmidt** in the adjacent park continues to be the domicile of the German federal president, the **Villa Schaumburg**, once the residence of the chancellor, now serves only representative purposes. It was here that Konrad Adenauer once resided, a monument to whom embellishes the new offices of the German chancellor. The wide street linking the governmental district with the town centre also bears the name of Konrad Adenauer. Passing the Ministry of Foreign Affairs and the E. M. Arndt House, it ends in the grounds of the court gar-

Palais Schaumburg, formerly residence of the Federal German Chancellor

dens – with the castle of the electoral prince and the municipal garden – at the Koblenzer Tor (Koblenz Gate). It is also on this level, just above the Kennedy Bridge, that the unique toll bastion "Alter Zoll" stands on the river Rhine, affording a splendid view.

The "Langer Eugen", the lower parliamentary house in Bonn.

Cologne

Even from a distance the visitor can recognise the unmistakable landmark of Cologne : the **Cathedral**, one of the most impressive edifices in the Occident, 144 metres long and 43.50 metres high above the central nave.

The St. Peter's Bell, 24 tons in weight and with a clapper which alone weighs 16 metric hundredweight, is the largest swinging bell in the world. The magnificent stained glass is a further superlative – the Cathedral has 1350 square metres of mediaeval windows. The **"Gero-Kreuz"** (Gero Cross) stands out from the host of unique art treasures.

This crucifix, donated to the Cathedral by Archbishop Gero in 976, is the oldest preserved large-scale sculpture north of the Alps. The **"Dreikönigenschrein"** (Shrine of the Magi) (1180–1220), weighing 6 metric hundredweight, is one of the world-famous treasures of the Cathedral. It contains the precious relics of the three saints and is considered to be an outstanding example of goldsmiths' work. The famous Cathedral picture, which today decorates the "Marienkapelle" (Chapel of St. Mary), is a masterpiece of the Cologne school of painters and Stefan Lochner, created around 1450.

The largest choir-stalls in Germany, consisting of 104 seats, were carved from oak around 1310.

The choir screen with its total of 42 pictures also dates back to about this time. The 144 Gothic figures on the high coir buttresses are especially graceful.

As if one such edifice were not enough, 12 other Romanesque churches form a circle around the Cathedral, irrefutable proof of the wealth of the town in the Middle Ages.

Together they established the reputation of Cologne as the "Rome of the North" or "holy Cologne". The oldest Romanesque church is the St. Pantheon, consecrated in 980.

It has the oldest preserved cloister in Germany.

As "Colonia Claudia Ara Agrippinensum", Cologne enjoyed Roman municipal rights as early as 50 AD. For 400 years it formed the north eastern cornerstone of the Roman Empire. It is therefore not surprising that Cologne can still show rich remains of Roman buildings, for example parts of the formerly 1 kilometre square town walls with their corner tower and north tower, parts of the underground canalisation system for the town drains and of the 80 kilometre long aquaduct which brought spring water to the town from the Eifel.

After Cologne had become an episcopal city as early as the 4th century, Charlemagne established the Archbishopric around 800. The archbishops, originally only advisers of the German emperors, became electoral princes and thus also secular rulers in the 10th century. Around 1220 they had the 6 kilometre long town walls built, so that the city, with space for approximately 40,000 people, became the then largest fortification in the world. The founding of the university (1388) gave even greater significance to the city, but after the discovery of America it lost to the seaports its major position as a trading centre.

It was this period of the city's zenith that brought forth not only the churches, but also the Romanesque **Overstolzenhaus** (13th century, Gothic wall paintings), the **"Gotisches Rathaus"** (Gothic Town Hall) (14th century) with its magnificent Renaissance hall and the Jewish ritual immersion bath (12th century) on the forecourt as well as the splendid Gothic structure of the **"Gürzenich"** (15th century), in which the town council used to receive emperors and kings. In the area of the old city centre the attentive visitor can still find – despite the ravages of the Second World War – more burghers' houses dating back to the 14th to 18th centuries and even older remains of the town fortifications with mighty towers and three preserved tower fortresses.

Cologne Cathedral (1248–1880): the visitor can enjoy a splendid panoramic view from the observation platform (95 metres) of the 157 metre high south tower.

▲ Cathedral forecourt

Market, Town Hall ▼

Old town and Cathedral ▶

Arsenal ▼

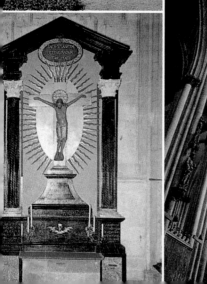

◀ *View from the Rhine Park*

bottom middle: Cathedral: Gero Cross

Cathedral: chancel interior ▼

The church of "St. Maria Himmelfahrt" (Assumption of the Blessed Virgin Mary), the most significant Jesuit construction in north-west Germany, dates back to the Baroque period. At that time also the famous painter Peter Paul Rubens was working in Cologne. Some of his paintings can be seen in the Wallraf-Richartz-Museum.

From 1794 the city was occupied by troops of the French revolution. Napoleon dissolved the archbishopric and confiscated the church possessions almost in their entirety – as was done everywhere in Germany. After Cologne had fallen to the Prussians in 1815 and was once again an archiepiscopal seat, there was a new economic boom. It was especially under the rule of Lord Mayor Konrad Adenauer (from 1917) that the city gained greater and greater importance, before the Second World War caused horrific damage : 95% of the old city centre was destroyed, the population figures fell from 800,000 to a mere 40,000. However, the reconstruction of the city was effected in an inimitable way in the Fifties and Sixties, restoring even the Romanesque churches. Present-day Cologne is one of the most important traffic centres in Europe, possessing as it does major railway lines, a link-ring of motorways, 8 bridges across the Rhine, a significant port for the transshipment of sea consignments and a modern airport. It is also the largest television and radio broadcasting centre in Europe, a trade metropolis of European standing and the location for headquarters of such world-renowned firms as Ford, Klöckner-Humboldt-Deutz and 4711, established on the outskirts. Throngs of visitors attend the trade fairs and congresses held in the city as well as its cultural facilities.

There are 9 city-owned museums and innumerable museums run by churches or private companies, but the outstanding examples among these are the **Wallraf-Richartz-Museum** (painting from the Middle Ages up to 1900) and the **Ludwig Museum** (Art of the Modern Times), which, together with the Philharmonic Concert Hall, are housed in a modern building between the Cathedral and the Rhine. The Hall of Art and 120 galleries complete the extensive range of facilities offered to the connoisseur of painting and sculpture.

Lovers of the theatre will find small stages and people's theatre groups as well as the Theatre and Opera House.

The **"Römisch-Germanisches Museum"** (Roman-Germanic Museum) offers a vast collection of exhibits from Roman culture on the Rhine.

Despite its metropolitan atmosphere, visitors to Cologne will also find romantic corners with taverns, pubs and inns, in which they can enjoy the famous "Kölsch" beer. The town is surrounded by two green belts. The outer one is 12 kilometres long and invites visitors to participate in active relaxation on its endless walks, in its stadions and on its many playgrounds with a lawn area for leisure activities. Cologne's reputation as "the green city" has also been confirmed by the modern 600 metre long tunnel which keeps the Rhine banks free of motor traffic.

Information

Tourist-Information Andernach, Läufstraße 11, 56626 Andernach.
Tel. 02632/922300"Altstadtfest" - 1. Wochenende im Juli; "Fest der 1.000 Lichter"
- 1. Wochenende im August; "Michelsmarkt" - letztes Wochenende im September.

Verkehrsamt Assmannshausen, 65385 Assmannshausen. Tel. 06722/2962

Stadtverwaltung Bacharach, Oberstraße 1, 55420 Bacharach. Tel. 06743/1297

Verkehrsamt Bad Breisig, Albert Märtel's Straße 11, 53498 Bad Breisig.
Tel.02633/97071

Kurmittelzentrum Bad Honnef, 53604 Bad Honnef. Tel.02224/184169-70

Verkehrsamt Bad Hönningen, 53557 Bad Hönningen. Tel.02635/2273

Verkehrsamt Bad Salzig, Oberstraße 118, 56154 Bad Salzig. Tel.06742/6297

Stadtverwaltung Bendorf, Im Stadtpark 1-2, 56159 Bendorf. Tel. 02622/703-173
"Drei-Städte-Wandertag" - Christi Himmelfahrt; "Krebbelschesfest" - letztes Wochenende im
August; "Burgen- und Parkfest" - erstes Wochenende im September.

Verkehrsamt Bingen, Rheinkai 21, 55411 Bingen. Tel.06721/184205

Tourist Information Boppard, Postfach 1661, 56140 Boppard. Tel. 06742/3888
"Rheinuferfest" - 3. Wochenende im Juli;"Tal total" - letzter Sonntag im Juli; "Zwiebelmarkt" -
2. Mittwoch u. Donnerstag im September.

Touristinformation Bonn, Münsterstraße 20, 53103 Bonn. Tel. 0228/773466

Stadt- u. Verkehrsamt Braubach, Rathausstraße 8, 56338 Braubach. Tel.02627/203
"Mittelalterlicher Handwerkermarkt auf der Marksburg" - Himmelfahrt-Donnerstag bis
Sonntag (alle zwei Jahre); "Rhein in Flammen" - 2. Samstag im August.

Verkehrsamt Brey - siehe Rhein-Mosel-Eifel Touristik Koblenz

Verkehrsamt Eltville, Schmittstraße 10, 65343 Eltville. Tel. 06123/5091

Ortsgemeinde Erpel, Frongasse 1, 53579 Erpel. Tel.02644/2570
"Sommerkirmes" - 3. Sonntag im Juni; "Weinfest" - 3. Sonntag im September.

Fremdenverkehrsamt Ingelheim, Neuer Markt , 55218 Ingelheim. Tel. 06132/782-0
"Rotweinfest" - Ende September/Anfang Oktober; "Internationale Tage" - Mai.

Verkehrsamt Kamp - Bornhofen, Rheinuferstraße 34, 56341 Kamp - Bornhofen.
Tel. 06773/360 "Backeskirmes" - eine Woche nach Pfingsten; "Heimatfest" und "Tal total" -
letztes Wochenende im Juni.

Städt. Verkehrsamt Kaub, Metzgergasse 26, 56349 Kaub. Tel. 06774/222
"Tal total" - letztes Wochenende im Juni;"Winzerfest" - 1. Wochenende im September.

Rhein-Mosel-Eifel Touristik, Bahnhofstraße 9, 56068 Koblenz. Tel. 0261/14024-6

Touristik- u. Congressamt, Postfach 2080, 56020 Koblenz. Tel. 0261/31304
"Altstädter Sommerfest" - 1. Wochenende im Juli;"Rhein in Flammen" - 2. Samstag im
August;"Weinfest" im Stadtteil Lay - letztes Septemberwochenende.

Verkehrsamt d. Stadt Köln, Unter Fettenhennen 19, 50667 Köln. Tel.0221/2213343

Tourist Information Königswinter, Drachenfelsstraße 11, 53639 Königswinter. Tel.
02244/889325 "Rhein in Flammen" am Siebengebirge - 1. Samstag im Mai;"Altstadtfest" in
Königswinter - 1. Wochenende im Juli.

Städt. Verkehrsamt Lahnstein, Postfach 2180, 56108 Lahnstein. Tel. 02621/175-
241"Heimatfest" - 2. Wochenende im Juli;"Rhein in Flammen" - 2. Wochenende im August;
"Oberlahnsteiner Stadtfest" - 2. Wochenende im September.

Verkehrs- u. Verschönerungsverein Leutesdorf e.V., 56599 Leutesdorf. Tel. 02631/ 72227 "Fest der Ortsvereine" - 3. Sonntag im Juni;"St. Laurentius - Kirmes" - 2. Sonntag im August;"Winzerfest" - 2. Sonntag im September.

Verkehrsamt Linz, Rathaus am Marktplatz, 53545 Linz. Tel.02644/2526
"Rhein in Flammen" - 1. Samstag im Mai; "Winzerfest - 2. Wochenende im September".

Städt. Verkehrsamt Lorch, Markt 5, 65391 Lorch. Tel. 06726/18-0

Verkehrsverein Mainz e.V., Bahnhofstr. 15, 55116 Mainz, Tel. 06131/286210
"Mainzer Fastnacht"; "Mainzer Weinmarkt" - letztes Wochenende im August; "Volksfest im Volks- u. Stadtpark" - 1. Wochenende im September.

Stadtverwaltung Neuwied, Kirchstr. 52, 56564 Neuwied. Tel. 02631/802-260

Verkehrsverein Niederheimbach, 55413 Niederheimbach. Tel. 06743/6077

Städt. Verkehrsamt Oberwesel,Rathausstraße 3, 55430 Oberwesel. Tel. 06744/1521
"Tal total" - letztes Wochenende im Juni; "Weinmarkt" - 2. Wochenende   im September;"Nacht der 1.000 Feuer" - 2. Samstag im September.

Touristinformation Stadt Remagen, Kirchstraße 6, 53406 Remagen. Tel.02642/22572
"Promenadenfest mit Rhein in Flammen"- 1. Maiwochenende.

Ortsgemeindeverwaltung Rheinbrohl, 56598 Rheinbrohl. Tel. 02635/2626
"Weinfest mit großem Winzerzug" - 1. Wochenende im Oktober.

Verkehrsamt Rhens - siehe Rhein-Mosel-Eifel Touristik Koblenz

Tourist Information Rolandseck, 53424 Rolandseck. Tel. 02642/22572

Verkehrsamt Rüdesheim, Rheinstraße 16, 65385 Rüdesheim. Tel. 06722/2962
"Tal total" - letzter Sonntag im Juni; "Der Rhein im Feuerzauber" - erster Samstag im Juli; "Rüdesheimer Weinfest" - 3. Wochenende im August; "Die Woche des Federweißen" - Ende Oktober/Anfang November, Weihnachtsmarkt im Advent.

Verkehrsamt Sinzig, Bäderstraße, 53489 Sinzig. Tel. 02642/42601
"Ahruferfest - Bad Bodendorf" -letztes Wochenende im Juli; "Kirmes" - Ende August/Anfang September; "Dorffest" - letztes Wochenende im September.

Städt. Verkehrsamt St. Goar, Heerstraße 86, 56326 St. Goar, Tel. 06741/383
"Fest der Fliegenden Brücke" - Ostermontag; "Tal total" - letzter Sonntag im Juni;"Schützen- und Heimatfest" - 3. Wochenende im Juli;"Int. Hansenfest" - 1. Wochenende im August;"Weinfest mit Rhein in Flammen" - 3. Wochenende im September.

**Städt. Verkehrsamt St. Goarshausen, Bahnhofstraße 8, 56343 St. Goarshausen.
Tel. 06771/427** "Fest der Fliegenden Brücke" - Ostermontag;"Tal total" - letzter Sonntag im Juni;"Weinwoche mit Rhein in Flammen" - 2.-3. Wochenende im September;"Winzerfest" - 3. Wochende im September;"Herbst- und Weinlesefest" - 3. Samstag im Oktober.

Verkehrsamt Spay - siehe Rhein-Mosel-Eifel Touristik Koblenz

**Verkehrs- u. Verschönerungsverein Trechtingshausen, 55413 Trechtingshausen.
Tel. 06721/6115** "Mai-Fest-Spiele" - Christi Himmelfahrt; "Tal total" - letzter Sonntag im Juni; "Rhein im Feuerzauber" - erster Samstag im Juli.

Städt. Verkehrsamt Vallendar, Rathaus, 56179 Vallendar. Tel. 0261/650391

**Kurbetriebe der Landeshauptstadt Wiesbaden, Verkehrsbüro Postfach 3840, 65028
Wiesbaden. Tel. 0611/1729780** "Internationale Maifestspiele" - während des ganzen Monats Mai; "Intern. Reit- und Fahrturnier" - Pfingstwochenende.